CALVINISM

CALVINISM

by
A. DAKIN, B.D., D.Theol.
President of Bristol Baptist College

DUCKWORTH
3 Henrietta Street, London, W.C.2

First Published 1940
Reprinted 1941, 1949
All rights reserved

PRINTED IN GREAT BRITAIN
BY JARROLD AND SONS LIMITED, NORWICH

PREFACE

CALVIN is recognized to-day as the creator of that aggressive type of Protestantism which played so large a part in the shaping of modern Western civilization. In addition to his distinctive contribution to theology, he gathered the Protestant doctrines into a comprehensive system, hammered out at Geneva an ecclesiastical order which produced Presbyterianism and influenced most other Protestant bodies, and also originated an ethical emphasis which gave tone to the life of the New World as well as the Old. All this is included in the term Calvinism. It is at once theology, organization and ethics.

The present volume aims at an exposition of the system that the reader may in some measure know what it is and what it produced. Only rarely have I attempted to indicate where criticism would arise from the modern point of view and the lines which such criticism might take.

I have followed the natural division of the subject, dealing first with the theology, then with the organization, and reserving certain specially interesting points for separate consideration. I am, of course, conscious of the inadequacy of the treatment, and indeed, of the difficulty of doing justice to so great a creative genius as Calvin, but I hope that the aim of presenting a useful introduction has been attained.

To me personally it has been a stimulating experience to read steadily through the *Institutes* and gain a

5

comprehensive view of the *summa* of Christian
theology. I could wish that the following study might
send others to the Reformer's monumental work, to be
brought in contact with his earnest spirit and feel the
mighty sweep of his thought.

The subject is timely if only because of the revived
interest in Calvinism which is a feature of current
theology. No one indeed can cast even a cursory
glance over the material without realizing that the
problems raised are living issues in the world of
to-day. If this is so, it is good to have presented to
us a system of thought in which solutions of these
problems are attempted, for even though the prof-
ferred solutions may have to be rejected, they at least
serve as the starting point for new thinking. Hence
the study of Calvinism at the present time is something more than a mere reading of the past, interesting
as that may be. History it is, but it readily passes
over into a challenge to us, as once again we face the
urgent task of creating a truly Christian civilization,
in which the glory of God and the good of man may
be achieved.

A. DAKIN.

March 1940

CONTENTS

PART I. CALVINISM AS A DOGMATIC SYSTEM

7

PART I

CALVINISM AS A DOGMATIC SYSTEM

CHAPTER I

THE TRUE KNOWLEDGE OF GOD

I. KNOWLEDGE OF GOD AND SELF-KNOWLEDGE

THE chief source of Calvinism as a dogmatic system is the *Christianae Religionis Institutio,* " Institutes of the Christian Religion." It was first published in 1536, then several times enlarged and re-issued till the final edition of 1559. Not the least merit of the book is that in the end its author made it as far as possible a complete handbook of Christian theology. It is not a discussion of a few important theological themes, as one might erroneously infer from the treatment of Calvin in many of the histories of Christian doctrine. Its aim rather is to give a complete theology to the Christian man, nor does its author ever lose sight of the unity of the whole. Indeed, in one or two sayings, he even goes so far as to suggest that he is putting forth not only the sum-total of theology but of philosophy also, and certainly all the knowledge that is necessary for salvation. He is consciously offering a world outlook, a complete system, and in his own mind there is a certain finality about it. The true and solid wisdom has been once for all revealed and he will now put it forth in a comprehensive way.

This breadth of outlook is not unlike that of mediaeval Scholasticism which regarded theology as the queen of the sciences and ever aspired to this same unity of thought. In this respect Calvin shared the outlook of his time. We are apt to forget that in reality the

Reformation position was only a modification of that of the mediaeval Church. The modification was tremendously important, and naturally historians have been obliged to emphasize the points of difference, justification by faith, for example, as against justification by works, or with Calvin the great stress on the doctrine of predestination. But we shall misjudge Calvin altogether unless we realize that he regards himself as putting forth the sum-total of true faith. He is expounding Christianity, not just certain aspects of it. Still less is he aiming at merely correcting a few errors. Everything pertaining to Christianity, he says, is contained in Scripture. It is this " everything " that he holds steadily before his mind and seeks to make plain.

Hence he not only takes up each separate Christian doctrine in turn, but relates each to each, and regards each in its relation to the whole. Thus he begins at the beginning and proceeds orderly to the end. A comparison with Melanchthon's *Loci* gives clearly the point of view. Nor was this systematizing tendency unimportant for Calvinism. It is, indeed, one of the factors making for its influence. The human mind craves such a unity, thought demands it, and Calvinism offered it. Thus the *Institutes* seeks to instruct the Christian fully both in his reading of the Scriptures and his understanding of the faith, and beyond such understanding there is little according to Calvin for the earnest man to trouble about.

He begins then with God and man confronting each other in the world of experience. How comes it that man wants a doctrine of salvation? And why is it necessary for men to concern themselves with spiritual matters?

Calvin's answer is that the demand is in the facts of life, especially in that activity of the human mind which gives us knowledge. Man is found knowing something of himself and also something of God. These two branches of knowledge are connected by many ties, nor is it easy to determine which of the two precedes and gives birth to the other. However clear it is that man cannot survey himself without turning his thoughts toward God. It is obvious that our endowments are not from ourselves, and also those blessings which increasingly distil to us from heaven are like streams conducting us to the fountain. Further the infinitude of good which resides in God becomes apparent from our poverty. The world of misery into which we have been plunged by the revolt of the first man, leads every man, stung by the consciousness of his own unhappiness, to obtain at least some knowledge of God. It leads him to know that in God is the true light and wisdom, solid virtue and exuberant goodness. Men rest in themselves only so long as they are ignorant of themselves, and they are entirely ignorant of God only so long as they rest in themselves. Every person on coming to the knowledge of himself is not only urged to seek God, but is also led as by the hand to find Him (I.i.i).[1]

This is Calvin's exposition of the thought that God has nowhere left Himself without a witness. The urge to religion is in the constitution of man, the creature being made for the creator. Consequently an analysis of human nature and human life, if carefully and accurately made, will not only show man's need of God but also how the Christian salvation meets that

[1] The references in the text are to the *Institutes*, the English edition by Henry Beveridge.

need and how God's grace operates. The fact of God is in the mind, thought presupposes enquiry concerning Him, and all such enquiry leads in the direction of Christian truth.

But how can one make this analysis and be sure of its accuracy? Calvin maintains that it comes straight from the knowledge of God and in no other way. Man can read the facts of life rightly only as he takes God as his starting-point. The idea seems to be that the natural man has enough light in him to make him in some degree realize the necessity of the knowledge of God but not enough to enable him to know either God or self correctly. So long as the mind is confined to this world and fails to look above there is no adequate light. Even for the true knowledge of self the knowledge of God is essential, for only in His righteousness, wisdom and purity can we know our unrighteousness and folly. " For such is our innate pride that we always seem to ourselves just, upright, wise and holy, until we are convinced by clear evidence of the contrary. Convinced we are not if we look to ourselves only, and not to the Lord also, He being the only standard by the application of which this conviction can be produced " (I.i.2). On this basis, then, the knowledge of God, bringing with it the only true knowledge of self, is both the starting-point and sum of human wisdom. Consequently we are left with the problem of how man can know God.

In a sense the *Institutes* as a whole is the answer to this question.

However we must note that Calvin is not primarily interested in the theoretic side of Christianity. Indeed one of the features of the *Institutes* is its strong practical bias. Hence it is made clear at the outset that the knowledge of God intended is such knowledge as may form the basis of true piety out of which religion springs. We have to know most of all what God means for us, what He is to our interest, as well as what is conducive to His glory. Thus it is not sufficient to hold that God is the only being whom we ought to worship. We have to discern also what benefits He can bestow, and be persuaded that He and He alone is the fountain of all blessings so that we may seek everything only in Him. For unless men place their entire happiness in God they will never yield up their whole lives to Him in sincerity and truth (I.i.2). The end is twofold—obedience and gratitude; the life framed in obedience to the divine will, and the mind ever gratefully ready to acknowledge that God is the source of all goodness. Hence it is not knowledge for its own sake, but entirely that men may be able to respond to the divine condescension and enter into true communion. Calvin will instruct unto salvation. Beyond that his interest does not go. The knowledge of God which he visualizes is that of St. John's gospel—knowledge leading to eternal life.

It consists of two parts—(i) the knowledge of God as creator, and (ii) the knowledge of Him as redeemer.

These form the two main divisions of the *Institutes*, and as we should expect, the second receives much fuller treatment than the first. In the one God's creative activity and providence are dealt with; in the second, the work of Christ, the revelation in Scripture, the work of the Holy Spirit, and finally the Church with the Word and sacraments.[1]

[1] For an analysis of the *Institutes* v. Appendix.

II. The Knowledge of God from Natural Religion

Calvin begins then by stating the fact of natural religion, as it is called, and then goes on to show its utter inadequacy.   Following St. Paul in *Romans* he feels the need of establishing the fact that all are without excuse, and, like the apostle, he does so by asserting that God is everywhere manifest and therefore can be known.   There is no nation so barbarous, no race so brutish, as not to be imbued with the conviction that there is a God.   Even those who in other respects seem to differ least from the lower animals constantly retain some sense of religion, so thoroughly has this common conviction possessed the mind, so firmly is it stamped on the breast of all men . . . a sense of deity is inscribed on every heart.   Idolatry itself is ample evidence of the fact (I.iii.1).   That is to say men know the existence of God as a truth of the mind.   With this idea each starts out on the career of life.   It is a doctrine not learned in any school, but one as to which every man is from the womb his own teacher.   Further it is a truth which nature allows no individual to forget no matter how much he may strive to do so (I.iii.3).

But not only the fact of God but also His nature and His perfections are revealed both in the world around and in the body and soul of man.   Here Calvin mentions astronomy, medicine and the natural sciences as affording many recondite proofs whereby the learned are able to take a loftier flight in their thinking and gain a right view of God's glory.   Yet even the illiterate peasant can find enough for the purpose.   The evidences are clear and are accessible to all. Moreover if these were not sufficient there is still the evidence of those works which are above the ordinary course of nature, the works of providence as Calvin calls them. " For in conducting the affairs of men He so arranges the course of His providence as daily to declare by the clearest manifestations that though all are in innumerable ways the partakers of His bounty, the righteous are the special object of His favour, the wicked and profane the special objects of His severity " (I.v.7). Calvin readily grants that there are surprises and difficulties, but he insists on this doctrine of rewards and punishments, and even on the possibility of men discerning the justice of it. He goes so far as to say that the divine wisdom is manifested in God conducting all things in perfect accordance with reason (I.v.8).

Both these lines of thought had influence on later Calvinism. For example there came a time when the study of astronomy particularly benefited from the fact that religious people regarded it as useful for inculcating piety and sustaining the devout heart. Theological students at one time were required to study it in order to enlarge, as was said, their conceptions of the deity. We may note in passing how Calvinism here touches the new spirit of science which was destined to become one of the creative factors of the modern world. There was as yet no conflict between science and religion. Rather science is the handmaid of religion, affording many proofs of God's witness to Himself. Consequently Calvin's followers were able to take an interest in new discoveries and ultimately to appropriate the gains of scientific knowledge. The more glorious and wonderful the world appears the brighter is the evidence of the glory

B

of God in creation. Thus science supports the teaching concerning natural religion.

The second idea, that of God's providence, had even greater influence, the more so because it was closely connected with the doctrine of salvation. In it Calvin was dominated by the Old Testament teaching of prosperity as the reward of righteousness and adversity the punishment of the wicked. This habit of thought went into Calvinism to have great effect later on both piety and action. Especially so when there was added to it the further idea that God uses means, including human instruments, to work out His providential government of the world. From such a position it is an easy step to the inference that the good man can, and indeed ought, to co-operate with God in punishing the wicked and rewarding the good. Thus the doctrine became a firm assumption in the theology. Adversity alone, Calvin maintains, is a sufficient proof of God's presence and activity, though besides being chastisement of the wicked it is also, as we shall see later, a salutary chastening of the elect.

However, though God is so plainly manifest in His works near and far, man all the world over has utterly failed to profit by the manifestation. Nowhere has the true knowledge of God been attained. Some lose themselves in superstition and others in wickedness. Since they do not conceive God rightly they come to worship phantoms, the dreams and figment of their own imaginings (I.iv.I). Thus superstition and idolatry are born to usurp the place of true religion. Further the blindness leading to superstition is always accompanied by stubbornness and pride, so that their folly cannot be excused. Still less can those be excused who err through deliberate wickedness, such as those who, hardened by a course of sin, turn away from all remembrance of God, even though it is prompted from within.

On this point of man's full responsibility for his failure to attain the knowledge of God from nature Calvin is insistent, as indeed he has need to be for the sake of his system. Though we are deficient, he says, in natural powers which might enable us to rise to a pure and clear knowledge of God, still, as the dullness which prevents us is within, there is no room for excuse (I.v.15). So again, " Man must bear the guilt of corrupting the seed of divine knowledge so wondrously deposited in his mind" (idem). At best, by the erroneous estimate which we inevitably form of nature, we either so obscure or pervert God's daily works as at once to rob them of their glory and their author of His praise.

So the argument runs. Man had the true knowledge close at hand in the world around, he utterly failed however to discover and take advantage of it, and for his failure he is solely and entirely responsible. What help then is there for him, and in what way can he ever attain to the knowledge of God?

Calvin here introduces the Scripture. This is the special revelation graciously given of God for the benefit of those whom He designs to bring into His fellowship.

We shall consider Calvin's doctrine of Scripture at a later stage. Here it is only necessary to point out that all his work rests on this foundation, so that every argument is buttressed with texts and expositions. Indeed the Reformer believed he was doing little more than opening up the Word of God. The Institutes itself is but a sustained commentary seeking to make clear just that revelation of God which is salvation for blind and erring men.

In the Scripture then the true God is manifest over against all the gods of the heathen. Broadly speaking He is there delineated in the same character as seen in His works. That is, first as creator and providential ruler. But also He stands here in relationship with men, thus appearing at the same time as redeemer. His attributes—those which it is most important for us to know—are His loving-kindness on which alone our safety depends; His judgment which is daily exercised on the wicked; and His righteousness by which the faithful are preserved. All this is made abundantly clear in Scripture to the end " that we may thereby learn to worship Him with integrity of heart and unfeigned obedience, and also to depend entirely on His goodness" (I.x.2).

III. The Biblical Doctrine of Creation and Providence

The Scripture presentation of God as creator makes explicit the two points already adumbrated in natural religion, namely, that He creates in the sense of bringing all things to birth, and secondly that He sustains by His continuous providence. As creator in the former sense He appears at the very opening of the Bible. The account in Genesis gives a clear manifestation of God's eternity in contrast with the creature and at the same time serves to refute the errors of speculation. It is a mirror wherein the divine goodness, power and wisdom are reflected. It shows that God created the world before making man thus having all things ready before man appeared. In this He displayed His liberality. The motive of creating was God's goodness, and man is the centre of the universe in the sense that all things were created for him. Before man angels had already been created. These too for the service of man.[1] The wickedness of bad angels and Satan was due to corruption and their falling away from God.

Then Calvin goes on to argue that the Scripture also teaches that of all the works of God, man himself is the noblest—the most admirable specimen of the divine justice, wisdom and goodness. Consequently we see the creative activity of God most clearly when we look at the nature of man. But to know man properly we must consider both his state before the Fall and his condition after—" for little would it avail us to know how we were created if we remained ignorant of the corruption and degradation of our nature in consequence of the Fall " (I.xv.1).

In creating man God deigned to animate a vessel of clay and make it the habitation of an immortal spirit (*idem*). Hence man consists of body and soul. That the soul is immortal is proved by the fact of conscience which responds to the judgments of God, by the fact that in each there is a sense of God, and also by all the noble features with which the mind is endowed. Thus man possesses intellect, ideas of rectitude, justice and honesty, memory and the gift of anticipation. All this endowment is gathered up in the phrase "created in the image of God." While it may be admitted that this phrase is not without reference to man's outward

[1] cp. Spenser's *Faerie Queen* II.viii.1.2.
They for us fight, they watch and duly ward,
And their bright squadrons round about us plant,
And all for love and nothing for reward.

appearance, yet the proper seat of the image is the soul. Here Calvin quotes Ovid, saying he would not vehemently oppose those who include this under the image of God, namely,

> Pronaque cum spectent animalia cetera terram,
> os homini sublime dedit caelumque videre
> jussit et erectos ad sidera tollere vultus.[1]

But he insists that the phrase " image of God " refers essentially to the spiritual, and if we wish to know truly what man's original state was we can only find it by seeing what man is like after being re-created in Christ. When we examine this we find that it consists in knowledge on the one hand, and true righteousness and holiness on the other. The image of God was manifest in the light of intellect, rectitude of heart, and soundness in every part. Intellect and will are the two chief parts of personality—intellect to enable us to discern between good and evil, and will to which choice belongs (I.xv.8).

All this however was so fearfully corrupted by the Fall that, though the image of God was not utterly defaced, yet there remained nothing but a ruin, confused, mutilated, and tainted with impurity (I.xv.4). This point is elaborated at greater length later in the treatment of the doctrine of original sin.

Then secondly, as God created so He sustains. Calvin is convinced that the Bible firmly establishes his doctrine of providence, and here there emerges that distinctive conception of God which is fundamental in the Calvinistic theology, even more important indeed than the doctrine of predestination, though

---

[1] *Metam.* I.84-6. Calvin shows a good knowledge of pagan literature which he does not hesitate to use—a reminder of his early humanistic studies.

this needless to say naturally and logically springs from it. Putting it in a word, we may say that Calvin conceives God primarily in terms of will. This supreme will is both law and activity. From it comes every decree and every divine action. It gives the law to man's life, and the fulfilling of that law is man's true way leading to God's glory. These points are brought out in a full exposition of the divine providence, which itself is regarded not merely as oversight, but far more as continuous and effectual activity.

First of all there is a general providence in which the creative activity of God is seen in the continuous protection and cherishing of the world. This is a point which is particularly the discernment of the godly, others being unable to see and accept it. God is " Governor and Preserver " not in the sense that He produces a kind of general motion in the machine of the globe and all its parts, but rather that by a special providence He sustains, cherishes, and superintends all things to the very minutest, even to the sparrow (I.xvi.1). Thus nothing happens fortuitously or is in any wise to be ascribed to fortune. Not even the sun rises and sets by a blind instinct of nature, but is governed by God in its course, that He may renew the remembrance of His paternal favour to us. The proof given is that it was stayed in its course at the prayer of Joshua (*Josh*. x. 3) and as a favour to Hezekiah its shadow receded ten degrees (2 *Kings* xx. 11).

So Calvin rejected decisively the idea that God's government means solely that He maintains in a general way the order of the universe. It must mean that He takes charge of each of His works, and even in the normal events of nature there is a particular providence as well as a general (I.xvi.1). Hence

everything can and must be ascribed to Him. He
raises the stormy wind, makes the storm a calm, smites
the people with blasting and mildew, ordains the
death of a merchant overtaken by robbers as well as
the flight of birds, divinely appoints the condition of
rich and poor, and so forth—all evidenced by quotations from Scripture (I.xvi.7). Thus the providence
is not just supervision but active energy extending
not less to the hand than to the eye. The argument
seems to be that as there are special movements of
nature obviously ordained of God and brought about
by Him for His special and particular purpose, so we
are bound to infer that all movements of nature are
similarly conditioned. The creation is new every
morning and renewed every evening, and the view
which maintains that all operates by a natural law
leaves no room for either the paternal favour or the
judgments of Almighty God (I.xvi.5).

This view of his, Calvin maintains strenuously, has
no connexion whatever with the Stoic doctrine of
fate. Indeed with the idea of fate he will have
nothing whatever to do. All the same his teaching
concerning providence would seem to lead to a
determinism as rigid as any in philosophy, even
though he so insists on ascribing everything to the
divine will. God is free, but there is little room left for
any real freedom of man. Indeed in some passages
God Himself is spoken of as though He also were
bound by His own decree. Thus—" we hold that God
is the dispenser and ruler of all things, that from the
remotest eternity, according to His own wisdom, He
decreed what He was to do, and now by His own power
executes what He decreed. Hence we maintain that by
His providence, not heaven and earth and inanimate

creatures only, but also the counsels and wills of
men are so governed as to move exactly in the course
which He has destined " (I.xvi.8).

Here we see the basis on which at a later stage in the
Institutes the doctrine of predestination will be made
to rest.

This decree of God is secret, a point which the
Reformer frequently emphasizes. There is in God an
inscrutable mystery, and the core of that mystery is
the divine will. That is to say, God's will is the ultimate
reality. We cannot examine it nor can we question
it. We can only discern and know it, and this in its
results.

It was at this point undoubtedly that Calvin was
able to ride off from his difficulties. Things that we
mortals cannot understand are in the deep mystery of
God, while any resentment on our part is just lack of
humility and ungodliness. Not once or twice in the
Institutes does the Reformer seem to the modern
reader to shirk the issue by simply falling back on this
idea of the inscrutability of the divine will. All
recognize of course that there must be an element of
mystery in God or He would not be God at all. So
far Calvin is justified. Still in the *Institutes* there is
no real appreciation of the problem of the world's evil
as a challenge to the divine goodness. A somewhat
naïve optimism was buttressed with the old idea that
all good fortune is blessing from God, and all adversity
and calamity the sign of His wrath. The doctrine of
providence was certainly not drawn from the close
examination of human experience, but is rather the
unfolding logically of an abstract idea. In this sense
it is theoretic. Once think of God as supreme will and
power only, and then try to work out His possible

relationship to the world, and some such solution as
Calvin's may not seem unreasonable. It only becomes
difficult when the facts of life themselves press upon
the mind. Yet experience shows that once men hold the
theory they can easily ignore many of the facts to
make the theory fit. This in part accounts for the long
reign of Calvin's idea. Luther also believed in the
divine providence, but whereas Calvin emphasized
God's wisdom and will, Luther gave such prominence
to the divine love and grace as to suggest a doctrine of
providence less logical perhaps and not less free from
difficulty, but certainly milder and more in accord
with the normal judgments of men. Calvin seems to
lack deep feeling for human suffering, at least in his
theological exposition. His doctrine is without pathos.

However we must not overlook the value of his conception. He had no idea of the stability of the universe
as indicated in the modern scientific conception of the
reign of law. Yet his thinking demands an equally
firm stability, his universe must be absolutely safe.
Calvin finds this stability in the sure and continuous
operation of the immutable will of God, which neither
changes nor relaxes ever its firm grip on the world of
events. " When the sky is overcast with dense clouds,
and a violent tempest arises, the darkness which is
presented to our eye, and the thunder which strikes
our ears and stupefies all our senses with terror, make
us imagine that everything is thrown into confusion,
though in the firmament itself all continues quiet and
serene. In the same way, when the tumultuous aspect
of human affairs unfits us for judging, we should still
hold that God, in the pure light of His justice and
wisdom, keeps all these commotions in due subordination and conducts them to their proper end " (I.xvii.1).

Of this fact there is for the elect at least an absolute assurance in the doctrine of providence coming to its climax in the idea of predestination. Thus if there is a sternness in the Reformer's teaching there is also a steadiness. Calvin himself finds it wonderfully comforting. It is for this he offers it. And if he thought of God as iron will he was thereby lifted above the shallow thinking and feeble sentimentalism which often accompanies the emphasis on God as love, and which certainly makes the world no more intelligible than the emphasis on will. He at least preserves in the divine the element of authority and supremacy, and if his God is a forbidding figure and seems so to later men, He was so no less to him, and we recall that Calvin and his colleagues lived a not unworthy life under the weight of this conception. Troeltsch maintains that this idea of God was a peculiar element of the Reformer's own piety ; he calls it " a unique product of Calvin's own mind."[1]

As always the Reformer's interest was truly religious and therefore he is at pains to make clear the advantages of his doctrine of providence. In doing so he reveals in part the motive that led to the insistence on it. The doctrine is necessary so that in success we may turn to God with thanks, in adversity may acknowledge His judgment. Only by recognizing the particular providence can we really understand and praise His omnipotence. That is to say the true knowledge of God demands this particular view of providence, because only this view and no other can be the ground of true piety. Indeed Calvin could not see how man could worship God at all unless he could

[1] *The Social Teaching of the Christian Churches.* Eng. Trans., vol. II, p. 583.

discern the divine activity in every event. When finally this conception was reinforced by the doctrine of election, so that a man could think of the divine decree as the ground and guarantee of his personal salvation, and when to it was added the further idea that all things are ruled for the benefit of the Church, even Satan and evil being over-ruled to the same end, obviously it became not a forbidding teaching but one of rich consolation and great moving power, at least for those who could think of themselves as elect. In this spirit the Reformer ends the discussion and also this section of the *Institutes* with a long meditation on the idea of providence, showing its relevance to the life of the pious and to the Church, and its importance both for right worship and true religion. The real difficulty, as later Calvinists found, was to win certainty of one's own election. Once that was clear and beyond doubt the consolation inevitably followed.

CHAPTER II

MAN'S FALLEN STATE

I. THE FALL AND ORIGINAL SIN

AFTER the knowledge of God as creator comes the knowledge of God as redeemer, and fundamental for this is the doctrine of original sin.

We have already seen that self-knowledge is necessary to wisdom, and also that only in the light of the knowledge of God can true self-knowledge be found. The natural man already knows himself as well endowed, but all such knowledge only puffs up and generates pride. Only when we measure ourselves by God, or contrast what we are with what we were intended to be, do we gain some knowledge of our miserable destitution and ignominy. Now this especially it is important for us to know, for this alone leads to humility before God and makes it possible for men to desire salvation. Thus by self-knowledge Calvin means primarily knowledge of sin and its effects in human personality. " Hence in considering the knowledge which man ought to have of himself, it seems proper to divide it thus, first to consider the end for which he was created, and the qualities—by no means contemptible qualities—with which he was endued, thus urging him to meditate on divine worship and the future life; and secondly, to consider his faculties or rather want of faculties, a want which when perceived will annihilate all his confidence and cover him with confusion " (II.i.3).

According to Calvin and indeed all the Reformers it

was necessary for man to be covered with confusion in
order that he might seek salvation from God and from
God alone; to be utterly without confidence in himself
or his ability so that his trust might be entirely in God.
Salvation by faith alone implies not merely distrust
of good works as a source of merit but also distrust
of all human ability. Man is utterly incapable of good
according to the theory. Therefore he must be saved
in some other way and by some other power.

Calvin, like Augustine before him, was able to
establish this essentially pessimistic view of human
nature by means of the doctrine of original sin. This
doctrine was of course no new discovery of the Reformation period. It was Catholic orthodoxy time-
honoured and universally subscribed. Only the
Reformation insistence on salvation by divine grace
alone as against the elaborate and legalistic system of
the Roman Catholic Church brought the old doctrine
into a new prominence. By sloughing off the huge
mass of mediaeval practices the Reformation reached
down again to the framework of that same mediaeval
structure, and thus brought to light in a new way this
old idea of original sin.

What was it then that could have so serious an
effect upon the sum-total of human life from Adam
to the end of time?

Calvin is surely right in insisting that, if the theory
is to hold, Adam's sin must be carefully specified. An
act which provoked God to inflict such fearful
vengeance on the whole human race could obviously
be no trivial offence but a heinous crime (II.i.4).
Hence he rejects as childish the common idea of
sensual intemperance. What happened was that
Adam provoked the wrath of God. The conditions in

Paradise were set to try Adam's faith and test his obedience. In both points he failed and fell. The beginning of the evil was pride, this led to disobedience, then to the despising of the truth, and finally to the turning aside to lies. When the Word of God is despised all reverence for Him is gone, and here pride, ingratitude and ambition took the place of reverence and worship. Then ambition opened the way for rebellion. Hence, and here is Calvin's characteristic touch, man carried away by the blasphemies of Satan did his utmost to annihilate the whole glory of God. " For our nature is not only utterly devoid of goodness but is so prolific in all kinds of evil that it can never be idle " (II.i.8).

We are familiar with all this from Milton's great epic. Milton transfers it all to Satan—ambition leading to rebellion and rebellion expressing itself in a life of ceaseless activity aiming at the annihilation of God's glory. The promoting of God's glory is the chief end of man, the purpose for which he was created. Sin then is doing the reverse. It is not merely indifference, but a continuous effort to pervert the whole order in heaven and earth—in a word, to undo the work of God.

Dante has a picture in the *Inferno*[1] where those guilty of simony are pushed head downwards into a sort of tube or chimney. One succeeds another, and as each goes down, fire rains on the soles of the upturned feet. It is a sort of inverted apostolic succession, the perversion of holy things. Calvin's idea of sin is similar. It is the complete reversal of the purpose of God in the creation, turning the cone as it were upon its apex. It is enmity against God,

[1] Canto XIX.

complete and vigorous. The key-word to the outlook
is " rebellion," another point of contact by the way
with Dante, who it will be remembered reserves the
lowest rung of hell for the arch-rebels against Church
and State respectively. We shall see later that the
corresponding doctrine to this idea of sin as ceaseless
activity against God is the insistence on the duty of
the Christian to be unwearied in his effort on behalf of
God. The stress on the idea of activity in both the
conception of sin and of the good life is an important
characteristic of Calvinism. It is related clearly to
the conception of will as the ultimate in personality
whether divine or human.

In seeking to track down the root of sin Calvin
gives an analysis of the Genesis story which, as we
read it, draws a smile at the marvellous array of sentiments, thoughts and purposes ascribed to primitive
Adam. But for the purpose of establishing the doctrine
of original sin logic demanded that the parent root
of sin should be found in the parent of the race. Here
we must discover the hard core of human intractability.
And it is the Reformer's merit that he sought this in
the realm of affection and will, in the inner disposition
rather than in some outward act. He sees it as an
activity of mind against the supreme mind. Consequently it remains an abiding state of the soul, and
therefore it is a soul-state which has to be dealt with
in the work of salvation. Thus like Paul, Calvin puts
the emphasis not on sins but on sin. He is working
with the concept which the apostle indicates in the
phrase " the carnal mind which is enmity against
God." This it is, with its effects in personality, which
from Adam is transmitted to the whole race.

To us it seems somewhat strange that Calvin, having

thus given a definition of sin which is essentially
spiritual, finding its origin in the human will, should
then regard such sin as capable of transmission from
Adam to all his descendants. In the earlier theories
where sin was thought of primarily as lust, it could
easily be conceived as a taint of the body passed on
in the act of generation. And that Calvin is still
under the influence of this type of Augustinian thought
is shown by his phraseology. He uses such terms as
" taint," " corruption," " vitiated." Nor apparently
does he feel the difficulty of a transmission of what is
essentially a failure of will. He rather avoids the
problem and this he can do the more readily through
his habit of emphasizing at every point the will of
God. Adam by sinning brought the death of the soul.
This reversed the situation for man. Adam was
punished by the withdrawal of his fine qualities,
wisdom, virtue, justice, truth and holiness, and by the
substitution in their place of those dire pests, blindness, impotence, vanity, impurity and unrighteousness (II.i.5). Then it was simply God's will that man
should be propagated in this lost state. " The cause
of the contagion is neither in the substance of the flesh
nor the soul, but God was pleased to ordain that those
gifts which He had bestowed on the first man, that
man should lose as well for his descendants as for
himself " (II.i.7). That is to say the Fall and its
consequences are in the divine decree as truly as is
the election. In fact the one rests on the other. Guilt
is from nature whereas salvation is from supernatural
grace, but both are ordained. It ought to be noted
here that there is no prominence given in all this
discussion to the idea of the solidarity of the race.
We are sinners not primarily because of the oneness of

C

mankind, but because God has willed that all men since Adam should be so born.

The actual definition given of original sin is " a hereditary corruption and depravity (pravitas et corruptio) of our nature extending to all parts of the soul, which first makes us guilty of the wrath of God, and then produces in us works which in Scripture are termed works of the flesh " (II.i.8).

In discussing this definition Calvin specially emphasizes that the effect is to be found in every part of our nature. Also that it is the real sin of each individual even though it has been transmitted.

On this latter point he writes—" Even infants bringing their condemnation with them from their mother's womb, suffer not for another's, but for their own defect. For although they have not yet produced the fruits of their own unrighteousness, they have the seed implanted in them. Nay, their whole nature is, as it were, a seed-bed of sin, and therefore cannot but be odious and abominable to God. Hence it follows that it is properly deemed sinful in the sight of God; for there could be no condemnation without guilt " (idem). Nor can we blame God for our condition or find refuge in the " daring presumption " odious to every pious mind, that God might have prevented Adam's fall (II.i.10). The sin is ours individually and the sin implies guilt.

Even at the time the obvious difficulties were voiced. How can there be individual guilt when the sin is transmitted? And again can there be a question of blame if all is decreed by God and none can escape the decree? These difficulties have never been resolved. Calvin himself troubled little about them, partly because he felt himself to be stating a doctrine

which was generally accepted as a major premise of
the Christian faith. But his statement did not by any
means leave the matter where he found it. His
penetration was deeper than that of most and his
logic more rigorous. By cutting sin loose from the
body and making it clearly a matter of the will he
involved theological thought in great straits to
maintain the old orthodoxy. He himself somehow
found his way through the difficulties, but inevitably
the ultimate effect of his statement was to weaken the
doctrine of original sin until theologians either abandoned it altogether or called for a new term to express
the element of truth contained in it. However it
cannot be too much emphasized that the doctrine
is fundamental in the Reformer's system, and it
passed into Calvinism to give colour to the thought of
generations of men. It helps to account for the
typical Calvinistic temper and outlook and is of course
one of the points where Calvinism is at variance with
the prevailing opinion of to-day.

II. The Enslavement of the Will

The conception of original sin carries with it the
virtual denial of the freedom of the will.

The doctrines of providence, of the enslavement
of the will, and of predestination—these, says
Doumergue, the biographer of Calvin, are the central
doctrines of the Reformation, and of these three that
of the enslavement of the will is the centre of the
centre.[1] As Doumergue indicates it was again a

[1] *Jean Calvin*, Vol. IV, p. 155. Personne ne contestera que les
trois doctrines de la Providence, du Serf-arbitre, et de la Prédestination ne soient, au moins en un sens, les trois doctrines caractéristiques
de toute la théologie des Reformateurs. Le Serf-arbitre, c'est le
centre du centre ; la Providence y aboutit ; la Prédestination en part.

position which Calvin shared with his fellow reformers. From the time when Luther made his position clear against Erasmus they all stood firm on the point and defended it as the very citadel of the faith. It seemed necessary so to defend it both against the Roman Catholic reliance on good works and also against the humanists and free-thinkers of the day. It was indeed the obverse side of the idea that there can be no salvation by works, or in other words, that since all is and must be of divine grace, then absolutely nothing can be the outcome of man's ability.

The background of the discussion even in the Reformation period was Pelagianism—the name goes back to Pelagius, a British monk of date about A.D. 400 against whom Augustine developed his doctrine of grace. Pelagianism in its extreme form asserted that in part at least man is able to live a good life by the aid of his reason, and for the rest the Church is there to instruct and enlighten. He has by nature both the will to good and the power, and all that religion needs to do is to add some measure of revelation to the knowledge already possessed, to show man what is right and what is wrong. Then it remains for man himself to follow the light as indeed he is well able to do.

Such a presentation of the matter naturally seemed to the reformers to lead straight to the idea of salvation by works and to eliminate altogether the need for divine grace. Hence they opposed it one and all. They deny entirely the natural man's ability either to know or to do. That is to say they ascribe to him a radical defect both of reason and will. In doing so they are fighting for their point of view that, as at the Fall man's nature was changed, so a further equally radical change is required to ensure salvation. A mere cure is not enough, there must be a new nature (II.i.9). Such new nature is the outcome of conversion. And conversion must be due entirely to the divine activity, otherwise pride takes the place of humility, and boasting in human power the place of rejoicing in God's goodness. As Calvin puts it, human virtue is totally overthrown in order that the power of God in man may be exalted (II.ii.1).

This view connects obviously with the idea of sin as already expounded, namely, that it is a soul-state, an attitude of mind, as against the Pelagian preoccupation with sinful acts. The reformers concern themselves chiefly with the inner life out of which all action springs. A good tree brings forth good fruit, and hence good works of every kind ought to be the spontaneous flowering of the new life within. But this means that the first requirement is that the new life should be there.

Thus there is an emphasis on the inward which is undoubtedly sound, and which was indeed at the time a valuable contribution to theological thought. It gives a right view of sin, and prepares the way for a true doctrine of salvation, marking clearly the distinction between morality as such and religion. As Doumergue puts it " Le bien, le mal, ce n'est pas une question d'acte, c'est une question de personnalité."[1] It was a gain that the reformers were thinking in terms of personality and that they turned both theological and philosophical thought in that direction. On the other hand it would be difficult for modern psychology to draw such a hard and fast line between the human and the divine and to set them in

[1] *Op. cit.* Vol. IV, p. 165.

such uncompromising opposition as Calvin's theory
seems to do. Nor would the modern man find it easy
to accept at its face value Calvin's estimate of human
freedom.

On this latter point the Reformer allows the definition which makes freewill consist in (1) a power of
reason to discern good and evil, and (2) a power of
will to choose the one or the other (II.ii.4). But he
then fixes the limits of this power of both reason and
will as existing after the Fall in such a way as to deny
any real ability to either—at least so far as concerns
the purpose of salvation.

It is axiomatic with him that every part of human
nature suffered at the Fall, but, as we have already
seen, he grants that some semblance of the image of
God persists. Both reason and will are corrupted but
not annihilated. They still remain essential parts of
personality only they no longer function for the purposes of man's higher good. Here Calvin follows
Augustine in holding that at the Fall there was the
corrupting of man's natural gifts and the complete
withdrawal of the supernatural. That is to say, all
things which pertain to the blessed life of the soul,
such as faith, love to God, charity towards one's
neighbour, and the study of righteousness and holiness, are extinguished until recovered by the grace of
regeneration. All these when restored to us in Christ
are to be regarded as above nature. But also, in
addition to this, soundness of mind and integrity of
heart were withdrawn, and it is this particularly
which constitutes the corruption of natural gifts
(II.ii.12). Man still has reason to distinguish him from
the brute beasts, some sparks which show that he is a
rational animal, but the light of this can no longer

shine forth with good effect. In the same way the
will also remains as an inseparable part of human
nature, but its soundness is so far impaired that it is
now incapable of even one righteous desire. Thus
though there is some residue of intelligence and
judgment and will left, yet since reason is blinded and
the will depraved, all that remains is " a shapeless ruin "
(*idem*).

In the consideration of reason the following points
are emphasized. First, it is obvious that in the mind
there is a love of truth and a desire of investigating
truth. But this love of truth fails before it reaches its
goal, immediately falling away to vanity. Secondly,
the mind labours under the defect of not knowing
what the knowledge is which it ought to study to
acquire. Hence it loses itself in the vain speculations
of idle curiosity. Calvin is never tired of asserting the
positive wickedness of such curiosity.

However he allows that apart from the purpose of
salvation, human reason when directed to inferior
objects is not without result, for to charge the intellect
with perpetual blindness so as to leave it with no
intelligence whatever is repugnant both to Scripture
and common sense (*idem*). Thus man being a social
animal knows by a natural instinct how best to preserve society. The minds of all have impressions of
civil order and honesty, the knowledge that societies
must be regulated by laws and so forth. Ideas of
equity agree in substance. All this is ample proof that
in regard to the present life no man is devoid of the
light of reason (II.ii.13).

So the force of human acuteness is displayed in the
manual and liberal arts. Everywhere there is evidence
of common capacity even though individuals differ in

their abilities. The capacity extends not merely to
the learning of the art but to the devising of something
new, or to the improving of that which has been
previously learned. So the admirable light of truth
in profane authors bears witness to the universal
endowment of reason, and should remind us that the
human mind however much fallen and perverted from
its original integrity, is still adorned and invested with
admirable gifts from its creator (II.ii.15). Thus Calvin
is able to wax eloquent in praise of the ancient law-
givers, philosophers, rhetoricians and writers on
medicine and the mathematical sciences, and later
to make use of such in his educational system. Only,
he urges, this gift must be ascribed to God, to whom
we should continually express our gratitude for it.
The Reformer will allow as much as possible to human
nature so long as it is denied the final ability of rising
to the higher knowledge.

This higher knowledge consists in three things, the
knowledge of God, the knowledge of His paternal
favour towards us, and the method of regulating our
conduct in accordance with the divine law. For these
there is no light of reason whatsoever. With regard
to the former two but more properly the second, men
otherwise the most ingenious are blinder than moles.
The philosophers it is true had some slight perception
of godhead but in no instance did it reach the goal.
To the great truths, what God is in Himself, and what
He is in relation to us, human reason makes not the
least approach (II.ii.18).

The will is in the same way equally ineffective. It
comes into play when there is a choice of two opposites
presented by the reason, but the epithets used in
Scripture for it show that the heart also is involved in

corruption so that in no part of man can integrity or knowledge or fear of God be found. The soul not only labours under vice but is altogether devoid of good (II.iii.2-3).

What then is the situation of those among the heathen who are admitted to have lived a good life? Are we to put Camillus and Cataline on the same level? Calvin answers that the virtues of such are special gifts of God which He distributes in diverse forms and in a definite measure to men otherwise profane. But, even here, in spite of the virtues, the heart itself is corrupt, and in any case, " the principal part of rectitude is wanting when there is no zeal for the glory of God, and there is no such zeal in those whom He has not regenerated by His Spirit " (II. iii.4). So virtues which may claim their meed of praise in civil society and the common intercourse of life have no value to establish a claim of righteousness before the judgment seat of God. We may recall that Dante had a similar problem with regard to the virtuous heathen and that neither could he assure them full salvation.

The will then is quite incapable of even the slightest movement toward good. Every such movement is the first step in conversion and this always in Scripture is ascribed to the operation of divine grace. But Calvin insists that not only is the will incapable but actually enslaved to sin towards which, he says, it inclines and hastens on with the strongest affection. Deprived of liberty it is led or dragged by necessity to evil (II.iii.5). Indeed such is the depravity of man that he cannot move or act except in the direction of evil. " Thus simply to will is the part of man, to will ill the part of corrupt nature, to will well the part of grace " (*idem*). God can only will good, Satan can only will evil, and corrupt man is like Satan " under a necessity of sinning." Thus the so-called freedom of the will has become a servitude to evil.

All this it is maintained is clearly shown if we turn to the work of salvation and note what the Spirit of God works in the regenerate man. It not merely assists the weak will but re-creates it (II.iii.6). If we ask what Calvin means by the phrase, the answer is that in conversion God turns the will from evil to good, so that man can now will the good and does so, and also has the power to move toward the willed goal. " God worketh in us to will " (Phil. ii. 13). Thus the very creation of the *good* will is the outcome of grace, and is and can be the possession only of the regenerate. This teaching Calvin believed to find both in Augustine and Scripture.

The summary of the matter would seem to be, that, at his first beginning, man was created with liberty of choice, that is, freedom to choose either good or evil (I.xv.8). After the Fall he lost this freedom of choice, his freewill being replaced not by constraint but by spontaneity. Without being constrained to it, but in virtue of the inevitable consequences of his sinful state, he spontaneously does evil. That is to say he no longer preserves anything but the freedom to evil.[1]

In this way Calvin believed himself able at one and the same time to deny the freedom of the will and yet retain the idea of human responsibility. The guilt is due to the fact that man sins voluntarily. His sinful nature is subject to the necessity of sinning, but it moves toward evil not by constraint but willingly, " by an affection inclined to it," or again " by a most

[1] Cp. Doumergue *op. cit.* Vol. IV, p. 170.

forward bias of the mind " (II.iii.5). Can it be said,
asks the Reformer, that man sins less voluntarily
because he is under a necessity of sinning? Calvin
apparently has no difficulty in answering. The
necessity is voluntary.

CHAPTER III

THE WAY OF SALVATION

I. THE PERFECT STANDARD OF RIGHTEOUSNESS IN THE LAW

THE doctrine of original sin has revealed the depth of man's need and also shown to some extent the kind of salvation that is required. This salvation is brought to us through Christ the mediator, and after the fall no knowledge of God without a mediator was effectual for salvation (II.vi.1). Indeed the Lord cannot be propitious to the human race without a mediator (II.vi.2). The recognition of this truth is the first step in piety which is the acknowledgment of God as Father, that is, as the one who defends, governs and cherishes us. Consequently Christ was held forth before the elect as the object of their faith and confidence from the beginning of the race (II.vi.4).

This necessity of Christ follows from Calvin's presuppositions. There is no adequate knowledge of God apart from revelation, the revelation is given in the Scripture, and according to Calvin's reading of Scripture Christ is the offered mediator both under the old dispensation and the new.

Three major questions then have to be faced:

(1) How Christ the mediator is exhibited to us. In brief, Calvin's answer to this is that he is shown to us both in the Law and the Gospel, i.e., in the Bible as a whole.

(2) How he is received. This leads to a discussion of

faith with its effects in the soul—the Christian life generally.

(3) How men are retained in the divine fellowship, a point which enables Calvin to deal with the Church and the sacraments.

These three points determine the main divisions of the *Institutes*.

Christ then is exhibited first under the old dispensation.

The whole system of religion delivered by the hand of Moses pointed to Christ in many ways and its sole value lies in its relationship to him. Its aim is to keep the Chosen People in suspense until his advent, to inflame their desire and confirm their expectation. This is true of all parts of the Old Testament.

Thus the ceremonial law is no better than the vain ceremonies of the heathen unless it is regarded with relation to the end in view. Its sacrifices foreshadowed the great sacrifice of Christ, the prosperity of David the kingdom of Christ, and the prophecies of the prophets the coming of Christ. So that in all respects Christ is the end of the Law.

In addition, the moral law unfolded in the Old Testament presents us with a perfect righteousness, nor can it be denied that the reward of eternal salvation awaits the perfect obedience of it (II.vii.3).

However the promise of salvation attached to the Law can never be realized because no one can perfectly obey it, so that nothing but instant death is presented by the Law. Does then God sport with us that He presents us with the prospect of eternal life but in conditions where it can never be attained? The answer is that the promise is realized in the Gospel, and the purpose of the Law is to make us desire this realization and seek it where it can be found. Thus the Law is a schoolmaster leading to Christ.

This it does, first, by exhibiting to us the righteousness of God, whereby every man is admonished of his own unrighteousness, thus destroying pride, self-love and all confidence in one's own ability. As in a mirror we discover any stains upon our face, so in the Law we behold, first our impotence, then in consequence of it our iniquity, and finally the curse as a consequence of both (II.vii.7). So by the Law is the knowledge of sin (*Romans* iii. 20).

This may well make the unbeliever rebellious, but it has the effect on the elect of spurring them on to reach out to the mercy of God in Christ. " Feeling how destitute they are, they take refuge in His mercy, rely upon it, and cover themselves up entirely with it; renouncing all righteousness and merit and clinging to mercy alone as offered in Christ to all who long and look for it in true faith. In the precepts of the Law God is seen as the rewarder only of perfect righteousness and the stern avenger of wickedness. But in Christ His countenance beams forth full of grace and tenderness towards poor unworthy sinners " (II.vii.8.)

The second office of the Law is to curb those who have no regard for justice and rectitude. Such persons are restrained not by any inward change but only by being made to refrain from external acts. Hence they are not on this account more righteous in the sight of God. On the contrary the more they are restrained the more they rage and boil and detest both law and law-giver. But this " extorted righteousness " is necessary for the good of society (II.vii.10).

Thirdly the Law (and this is its principal use) instructs believers in whom the Spirit of God is already working. " It is the best instrument for enabling them daily to learn with greater truth and certainty what that will of the Lord is which they aspire to follow, and to confirm them in this knowledge; just as a servant who desires with all his soul to approve himself to his master, must still observe, and be careful to ascertain his master's dispositions that he may comport himself in accommodation to them " (II.vii.12). None can regard himself as being so wise as to be free from this necessity. Thus by daily instruction in the Law we advance to a purer knowledge of God's will while at the same time the will to holiness is stimulated and excited to obedience. Thus the Law acts as a whip to the flesh urging it as men do a lazy sluggish ass (*idem*).

On these grounds Calvin repudiates those who discard the Law of Moses as being superseded by the Gospel. If we are to have a proper rule of life, he urges, it would be impious to discard this which contains " a perfect pattern of righteousness " (II.vii.13). The error of such people arises through failure to distinguish what has been abrogated in the Law and what remains. The ceremonies it is true, are no longer required, Christ having fulfilled the promise to which they pointed. But the moral law still stands and still presents the demands of God. Only its power of constraining the conscience is now no longer operative for Christians. We have to be freed from the fetters of the Law even while we look to the Law. That is, we are no longer under the fear of death because of our inability to fulfil the Law, though it remains an indubitable truth that the Law has lost none of its authority but must always receive from us the same respect and obedience (II.vii.15). Like the

Gospel it is a gift of God for the purpose of leading men to the goal. As such it is therefore to be accepted and revered by those knowing Christ from the Gospel as well as by those who preceded him.

It was committed to writing that it might thus teach us both the knowledge of God and of ourselves. As to the first, it inculcates a sense of awe before the divine majesty and binds us to His service, shows Him as Ruler and Father, and reveals the fact that righteousness is pleasing to Him and iniquity an abomination, thus urging on us the duty of seeking the one and shunning the other. Then with regard to ourselves it lays bare our utter powerlessness, makes us ashamed, and induces us to seek true righteousness not in ourselves but in God. The promises likewise attached to the Law, limited not to this world but embracing also things heavenly and eternal, reveal God's purity and love of righteousness and also His lovingkindness to us. Thus the Law taken all in all is a full revelation of the divine.

The nature of the moral law is illustrated by a detailed exposition of the two tables, the one dealing with our duty to God, the second our duty to our neighbour.

The first commandment calls away from all idolatry and superstition to the sole worship of the true God. It teaches us to give Him His due, namely adoration with its accessory, spiritual submission of conscience, trust, invocation, and thanksgiving (II.viii.16). The second commandment teaches us to offer only that spiritual worship which God has ordained, unpolluted by superstitious rites. The third, not to take the name of God in vain, insists, on its positive side, that we give God the glory that is His due, letting every thought and word bespeak His excellence. The fourth commandment speaks of a sabbath-rest prefiguring the spiritual rest of the people of God. There is, says Calvin, no commandment the observance of which the Almighty more strictly enforces. " We must rest entirely in order that God may work in us. We must resign our own will, yield up our heart, and abandon all the lusts of the flesh. In short we must desist from all the acts of our own mind that God working in us, we may rest in Him " (II.viii.29). The Jewish Sabbath is abrogated in Christ, and since Christians are now buried with him in baptism and risen to newness of life and are perpetually resting in God, they ought not to have anything to do with " a superstitious observance of days " (II.viii. 31). However while the Sabbath in this sense is done away, there is still room for Christians to assemble on stated days for worship and also to grant their servants relaxation from labour. This however is most fittingly observed on the Lord's day.

The fifth commandment enjoining duty to parents, implies submission to all set in authority over us whether they are deserving or otherwise. By conferring their station upon them the Almighty has shown that He would have them honoured. Hence we must yield them honour, gratitude and obedience, and the degrees of dignity ordained of God must be held inviolable (II.viii.36).

The commandment " Thou shalt not kill" prohibits all violence and injustice and every kind of harm from which our neighbour's body might suffer because God has bound the race by a kind of unity, and the safety of all is the charge of each. Hatred and wrath are condemned, and since man is created in the

D

image of God, we must hold the person of each sacred. Murder is prohibited, and indeed even so much as the wish and design for another's ill. There is no discussion at this point of the question of taking life in war or in the interests of the State.

The seventh commandment prohibits all unchastity. The eighth all lying and deception and all attempts at dishonesty, while at the same time it enjoins on us the fulfilling of our whole duty to others.

The ninth commandment forbids us to tarnish our neighbour's reputation with falsehood, and on the positive side enjoins us to keep it untarnished as far as truth will permit.

Finally the tenth commandment calls for a mind which is not prompted in the slightest degree contrary to the law of love. Not only must nothing of our neighbour's be coveted, but the mind must be free from all evil design on him, and further must be full of good towards him. The mind is to be regulated in much the same way as previous commandments seek to regulate one's actions.

Thus for Calvin the whole Law is summed up in the two commandments on which obviously his exposition of the decalogue is based, namely, love to God and love to one's neighbour. First our mind must be completely filled with love to God and then this love must forthwith flow out toward our neighbour (II.viii.51). Thus true piety and charity make up the Christian ethic. Of these piety comes first and is the root of charity. " Wherefore if we would hold the true course in love, our first step must be to turn our eyes not to man, the sight of whom might oftener produce hatred than love, but to God, who requires that the love which we bear to Him be diffused among all mankind, so that our fundamental principle must ever be, Let a man be what he may he is still to be loved because God is loved " (II.viii.55).

This note is very important for the understanding of Calvinism, namely, that Christian humanitarian sentiment is not based on any observation or judgment concerning man but is closely connected with the Christian's conception of God. That is to say there is a theological basis for it. The main emphasis in the system is love to God. Piety is primary and is indeed the ground of Christian ethics.

We note in passing that in this view of the Law as a sort of epitome of the Gospel Calvin gives the Old Testament a very important place which colours inevitably his whole conception of the Christian life. Those, he says, who search merely for dry and meagre elements in the Old Testament fail altogether to understand its end. It looks toward the fulfilment of righteousness that man may form his life on the model of the divine purity. For therein God has so delineated His own character that anyone exhibiting in action what is there commanded would in some measure exhibit a living image of God (II.viii.51).

II. THE MEDIATION THROUGH CHRIST

How then can man attain to this standard of righteousness presented in the Law and demanded of him by God? He is not only incapable of good but has also incurred the divine wrath by his guilt. In what way then can he stand before God at all?

The answer is that God Himself has provided a mediator—Jesus Christ. He was there even in Old

Testament days inspiring and helping the fathers, but now in the Gospel he is fully revealed and God's plan of salvation is made fully known. If we ask why this particular plan, we learn that it " flowed from the divine decree " (II.xii.1).

The mediator must of necessity be both God and man because no other can do the work required of him. Even if man had remained free from taint he was yet of too humble a condition to penetrate to God without a mediator. Hence God Himself must descend to us since we cannot ascend to Him. Who but a Son of God could restore us to the divine favour so as to make us, instead of sons of men sons of God, instead of heirs of hell heirs of the heavenly kingdom? Who could swallow up death but life itself? Who could conquer sin save righteousness?

" Therefore God in His infinite mercy, having determined to redeem us, became Himself our redeemer in the person of His only begotten Son " (II.xii.2).

Equally it was necessary that the mediator should become man to receive what is ours so as to be able to transfer to us what is his. He is spoken of as flesh that we may know that he is near to us, and since a principal part of his work is to reconcile us to God, opposing obedience to our disobedience, paying the penalty of sin and satisfying the justice of God, it was necessary for him to assume our nature and be of our stock. " Therefore our Lord came forth very man, adopted the person of Adam and assumed his name that he might in his stead obey the Father; that he might present our flesh as the price of satisfaction to the just judgment of God, and in the same flesh pay the penalty which we had incurred " (II.xii.3). He united the human and the divine natures that he might subject the one to death and with the other gain us the victory. Thus whoever would rob Christ of either his divinity or his humanity detracts from his majesty and obscures his goodness.

The actual union of the two natures is a great mystery and Calvin deprecates curious enquiry and speculation concerning it. He insists however that the two natures are both real. " He who was Son of God became son of man, not by confusion of substance, but by unity of person. For we maintain that the divinity was so conjoined with the humanity, that the entire properties of each nature remain entire, and yet the two natures constitute only one Christ " (II.xiv.1). This is analogous to the compounding of body and soul in man, each of which is separate, yet when compounded form one personality. The proof of Christ's nature is found of course in Scripture, and the heresies of the Nestorians and Eutychians and especially Servetus are refuted (II.xiv.2-8).

As mediator Christ fulfils the offices of prophet, priest, and king—all summed up in the term Messiah. It was Calvin apparently who first brought this fruitful idea of the three-fold office into dogmatics.[1]

As prophet Christ brings the full revelation which had been foreshadowed in Old Testament days. His revelation therefore is the fulfilment and completion of all the Old Testament prophecies, and in the doctrine which he delivered is substantially a wisdom perfect in all its parts. By his anointing (*Isaiah* lx. 1–2) he is distinguished from all other teachers, and moreover this anointing was not for himself alone but for his

[1] *v.* R. S. Franks : *A History of the Doctrine of the Work of Christ* Vol. I, p. 441.

whole body, that a corresponding efficacy of the Spirit might accompany the preaching of the Gospel (II.xv.2).

As king he is the eternal governor and defender of his Church. Thus he fulfills the ancient promise made to David that his throne should be established for ever. The old kingdom is revived and continued now in the Church, and Christ is armed with eternal power so that the perpetuity of the Church is thus effectually secured. Hence in all times of oppression and persecution, believers are animated with hope, being reminded that however numerous and powerful the enemies who conspire to assault the Church, they are not possessed of sufficient strength to prevail against the immortal decree by which God appointed his Son eternal King (II.xv.3).

Also the kingship guarantees to believers themselves victory in life culminating in immortality. The happiness promised consists not merely in external advantages such as leading a tranquil life, wealth and so forth, but belongs essentially to the heavenly life. " As in the world the prosperous condition of a people consists partly in the abundance of temporal goods and domestic peace, and partly in the strong protection which gives security against external violence; so Christ also enriches his people with all things necessary to the eternal salvation of their souls and fortifies them with courage to stand unassailable by all the attacks of spiritual foes. Whence we infer that he reigns more for us than for himself " (II.xv.4). Thus we are able to live patiently under every kind of hardship and to contend intrepidly with the devil, sin, and death, sure that we shall always be victorious. As God governs and cherishes the world, so Christ his people and the Church.

In the order of priest the mediator procures for us the favour of God. God could not be propitious to us without the expiation of sin. Christ offers such in his death which wipes away our guilt and makes satisfaction for sin. Thus he won for us access to God which he now secures for us by his perpetual intercession.

So we come to the doctrine of the atonement.

The Reformer begins by asking in what sense it can be said that God was our enemy until He was reconciled to us by Christ. So, he maintains, it is stated in Scripture. He gives two reasons. First to make us realize our estate. " Such modes of expression are accommodated to our capacity that we may the better understand how miserable and calamitous our condition is without Christ. For were it not said in clear terms that divine wrath, vengeance, and eternal death lay upon us we should be less sensible of our wretchedness without the mercy of God, and less disposed to value the blessing of deliverance " (II.xvi.2).

Then secondly, such statements are true because God who is perfect righteousness cannot love the iniquity which He sees in all. By reason of our corrupt nature and the depraved conduct following it we are offensive to God, guilty in His sight, children of hell (II.xvi.3). But as the Lord wills not to destroy in us that which is His own He still finds something in us which in kindness He can love. For though sinners we are still His creatures and created for life. Consequently mere gratuitous love prompts Him to receive us into His favour. Since however we cannot be received as sinners, God the Father anticipates our reconciliation in Christ (II.xvi.3). It is because He first loved us that He afterwards reconciles us to

Himself. Since this is done in Christ we must fix our eyes on Christ alone.

Calvin is at this point careful with Augustine to insist that the whole plan of salvation is the outcome of God's love. It is not as though the Father, hating us, was first moved to love us by the reconciliation wrought by Christ. Rather God the Father loved us even when He hated us—so it is put. He loved us before the foundation of the world, before we were anything at all, that with His only begotten Son we too might become sons of God (II.xvi.4).

If we ask in what way Christ purchased our righteousness Calvin answers, "By the whole course of his obedience" (II.xvi.5). He began to pay the price from the moment when he assumed the form of a servant, although a special emphasis falls, as in Scripture, on his death. The first step in his obedience was his voluntary subjection. He offered himself and that spontaneously. It was done not without struggle because he had assumed our infirmities. And says Calvin, it was no ordinary example of incomparable love towards us to struggle with dire terrors and amid fearful tortures, to cast away all care of himself that he might provide for us (*idem*). His subjection was entirely to the Father's will. He submitted to be condemned so that he might sustain the character of an offender and evil doer. Had he been slain, for example, in a seditious tumult there would have been no satisfaction in such a death. He had to die as a criminal. So he died between the transgressors. Yet by the same judge Pilate he was declared innocent. So Calvin writes "Our acquittal is in this, that the guilt which made us liable to punishment was transferred to the head of the Son of God" (*Is.* liii. 12).

This substitution we must remember in order to derive consolation from the fact that the just vengeance impending over us " the Son of God transferred to himself " (*idem*).

So death on the cross—the mode of it, indicates that he submitted to the curse. Not that we are to understand that he himself was overwhelmed, but that by enduring it he repressed, broke, annihilated all its force. Hence the cross, the symbol of ignominy, was converted into a triumphal chariot (II.xvi.6).

In contemplating all this we must never lose sight of sacrifice and ablution. Christ was a victim and his blood was shed. His blood thus became available both for propitiation and as a laver to purge our defilements (*idem*).

If now we take up in turn the phrases of the Creed we begin to see in its fullness the nature of the salvation wrought for us by Christ. Thus the phrase " he died " signifies that he placed himself in the power of death which held us under its yoke, that he might exempt us from it. But here again he died not in the sense that he was engulfed in the abyss of death, but rather that he destroyed it as it must otherwise have destroyed us. The result to us is that we are now emancipated from death so that it no longer has power over us. Also it means that by fellowship with him we experience the mortification of our earthly members, the death of the " old man." In his burial we too are buried to sin. So that the death and burial of Christ together signify the twofold blessing of deliverance from the power of death at the end and mortification of the flesh during our earthly life.

The descent into hell—in the Creed but not in Scripture—contains a vital truth. Calvin interprets it as evidence that Christ felt the full weight of divine

vengeance. Nothing would have been accomplished
had he died only a death of the body. What was
required was that he should engage at close quarters
as it were with the powers of hell and the horrors of
eternal death. Thus the phrase indicates " invisible
and incomprehensible judgment " which he endured
before God, to teach us that not only was the body of
Christ given up as the price of our redemption, but
that " he bore in his soul the tortures of condemned
and ruined man " (II.xvi.10). Thus the cry *My God,
My God, why hast thou forsaken me* was the expression
of his inmost anguish.   " And certainly no abyss
can be imagined more dreadful than to feel that you
are abandoned and forsaken of God and not heard
when you invoke Him, just as if He had conspired
your destruction " (II.xvi.11). However, says Calvin,
we do not insinuate that God was ever hostile to him
or angry with him. But he bore the weight of the
divine wrath and experienced all the signs of an angry
and avenging God (*idem*). So we ought to be no more
ashamed of the agony of Christ than of his cross. If
he had suffered only in body he would have been a
redeemer of bodies only.

Next the resurrection. This guarantees the victory
of our faith, being the proof that Christ has indeed
conquered death and gained the victory over sin. It
brings the restoring to righteousness and life, and the
divine power by which God maintains our faith is
most conspicuous in it. Whenever death is mentioned
resurrection is included and vice-versa. If death
speaks of the mortification of our members so resurrection of the renewal unto righteousness. It is also
the promise and assurance of our own personal
resurrection to eternal life,

The ascension denotes the beginning of the reign of Christ. He departed that he might be more useful to us, that his power might be more fully diffused in heaven and earth. Thus the words " sitteth at the right hand of God " mean that he has been installed in the government of heaven and earth, admitted to the administration committed to him, to continue in it till he descends to judgment. The end is that all creatures in heaven and on earth should reverence his majesty, be ruled by his hand, and do implicit homage by submitting to his power (II.xvi.15).

The advantages to the faithful of Christ's exaltation are that the kingdom of heaven, shut in Adam, is now opened again for all believers. We are now already seated in heavenly places, not entertaining a mere hope of heaven but possessing the earnest of it in our hearts. Further he is the advocate and intercessor in the presence of the Father, directing attention to his own righteousness so as to turn it away from our sins. Thirdly, it enables faith to know its own power on which depends strength for the triumph over hell. Christ then occupies his exalted seat that he may quicken us to spiritual life and sanctify us by his Spirit, and adorn his Church with all graces, preserving it from all its enemies (*idem*).

Lastly, he will come to judgment, and faith is encouraged to meditate on his last visible appearance on the earth, when he will appear to all with the ineffable majesty of his kingdom, the splendour of immortality, the boundless power of divinity and an attendant company of angels. However he will not ascend the judgment-seat for the condemnation of Christians but on the contrary they will share with him the honour of judging (II.xvi.18).

The whole of our salvation, then, as summed up admirably in the Apostles' Creed, is seen to be comprehended in Christ. It remains only to say that we must beware of deriving even the minutest portion of it from any other quarter. " If we seek salvation we are taught by the very name of Jesus that he possesses it ; if we seek any other gifts of the Spirit we shall find them in his unction; strength in his government; purity in his conception; indulgence in his nativity in which he was made like us in all respects in order that he might learn to sympathize with us; if we seek redemption we shall find it in his passion; acquittal in his condemnation; remission of the curse in his cross; satisfaction in his sacrifice; purification in his blood; reconciliation in his descent to hell; mortification of the flesh in his sepulchre; newness of life in his resurrection; immortality also in his resurrection; the inheritance of a celestial kingdom in his entrance into heaven; protection, security and the abundant supply of all blessings in his kingdom; secure anticipation of judgment in the power of judgment committed to him " (II.xvi.19).

CHAPTER IV

THE APPROPRIATION OF SALVATION THROUGH CHRIST

I. THE HOLY SPIRIT AND FAITH

So far we have followed Calvin in his consideration of the knowledge of God as creator and then as redeemer. This latter brought us to the fact of Christ as the sole mediator. Now we come to the section where he deals with the way in which we obtain the grace available for us in Christ, with a consideration of the benefits it confers and the effects that follow from it. Stated briefly the salvation is ours by reason of the secret operation of the Holy Spirit of God within us, and by our faith. The teaching concerning faith includes the treatment of the subject of repentance and this leads in turn to the characteristic reformation doctrine of justification by faith. Prayer is dealt with as the principal exercise of faith. Then at this point Calvin brings forward his doctrine of election since saving faith is not given to all but only to such as the Lord favours.

How then do we become possessed of the blessings which God has bestowed upon Christ for our good? The answer is—by Christ becoming ours and dwelling in us. Christ is possessed of the Holy Spirit in a special manner. Hence it is by the operation of this Spirit—ours through the indwelling Christ—that we are able to share the life and gifts of Christ and thus appropriate the salvation of God.

Faith is defined by Calvin as " a firm and sure knowledge of the divine favour towards us, founded on the truth of a free promise in Christ, and revealed to our minds and sealed on our hearts by the Holy Spirit " (III. ii. 7).

Thus the Reformer is emphatic in making faith consist, as he says, not in ignorance but in knowledge (III.ii.2), not in the submission of the understanding as the Roman Catholics demand; rather faith is conjoined with understanding as the Scripture uniformly teaches (III.ii.3).

But what is it then that one has to understand in order to be in a state of faith? If Calvin makes faith consist in knowledge he is quite clear in stating the kind of knowledge which he has in mind. It is, as we have already gathered from the previous exposition, solely the knowledge of God and moreover the knowledge of God in His saving purpose in Christ. In a word the knowledge of God as redeemer. It is not sufficient to know that God is, or even what He is in Himself. The important thing is the discernment of His will toward us, or in other words " in what character He is pleased to manifest Himself to us " (III.ii.6). That is to say faith so defined is the knowledge of the divine will in regard to man as revealed in the Word.

But here again, since the heart of man is not brought to faith by every word of God, we have further to consider what it is in the Word that faith properly has respect to. We find it is that especially which leads men to seek God rather than to shun Him. Shall we then, asks Calvin, for " will " which is often the messenger of bad news and the herald of terror, substitute the " benevolence " or " mercy " of God. He answers his question by saying that in so doing we surely make a nearer approach to the divine nature, " for we are allured to seek God when we know that our safety is treasured up in Him; and we are confirmed in this when He declares that he studies and takes an interest in our welfare " (III.ii.7). At this point there is required a promise to this effect, for on such a promise alone can the heart of man rely. This promise is given in the Word and particularly in Christ—the one pledge of divine love.

So we see that faith is that knowledge of God as saviour which alone leads man to trust Him for safety and all good. Such knowledge is absolutely bound to the Word and therefore without the Word faith cannot be. Since this means that it is bound to the revelation made in Christ it can be described as consisting in the knowledge of Christ. God loves no man out of Christ (III.ii.32), and the only way in which faith reconciles us to God is by uniting us with Christ (III.ii.30).

All this however is but the half of the matter. Faith is not merely the knowledge of God but also the embracing of that knowledge by the mind. To know the promises is one thing, to embrace them inwardly and make them ours is another. In this alone is engendered that confidence which we call peace. That is to say the final effect of faith is a firm trust in the salvation of God resting on the goodness of God on the one side, and our ability to accept that which certifies this goodness on the other. Thus there is a reciprocal action of personalities, and that is no faith which fails to lead a man truly to rest in God.

But since this is so, then, it is necessary to exclude a knowledge mingled with doubt, which so far from being firm is continually wavering. Just as the mind, blinded and darkened, is unable to rise to the proper knowledge of God's will, so the heart likewise fluctuating with perpetual doubt is equally unable to rest secure in such knowledge. Hence in order that the Word of God may gain full credit in us, both the mind must be enlightened and the heart confirmed from some other quarter (III.ii.7). This is the work of the Holy Spirit who is both the originator and the sustainer of faith. A simple external manifestation of the Word, it is true, ought to be sufficient but, such is the proneness of our mind to vanity, that unaided it can never adhere to the truth of God, and such its dulness that it is always blind even in the light. Hence without the illumination of the Spirit the Word itself has no effect; and hence it is obvious that faith is something more than mere understanding. Nor is it sufficient for the mind to be illumined by the Spirit of God unless at the same time the heart also is strengthened and supported by his power (III.ii.35). Thus the Spirit has a double operation. He purifies the mind so as to give it a relish for divine truth, and afterwards establishes it therein. " The word is not received in faith when it merely fluctuates in the brain, but when it has taken deep root in the heart and become an invincible bulwark to withstand and repel all the assaults of temptation. But if the illumination of the Spirit is the true source of understanding in the intellect, much more manifest is his agency in the confirmation of the heart, inasmuch as there is more distrust in the heart than blindness in the mind and it is more difficult to inspire the soul with security than to imbue it with knowledge. Hence the Spirit performs the part of a seal, sealing upon our hearts the very promises the certainty of which was previously impressed upon our minds " (III.ii.35).

In accordance with this view of faith it follows that

only the elect can possess it. The reprobate in spite of all appearances to the contrary are not able to penetrate to the secret revelation which Scripture reserves for the elect alone. On the other hand the seeming doubts of believers fail to affect the reality of their faith. Calvin admits that believers are frequently assaulted with terrors and disquietude. "When we say that faith must be certain and sure we certainly speak not of an assurance which is never affected by doubt, nor of a security which anxiety never assails; we rather maintain that believers have a perpetual struggle with their own distrust, and are thus far from thinking that their consciences possess a placid quiet, uninterrupted by perturbation" (III.ii.17). Yet however much they are assailed they never really abandon their sure confidence in the mercy of God. The truth is, unbelief does not actually reign in the hearts of believers, but only assails them from without, does not wound them mortally with its darts but at the most gives them a wound which can be healed (III.ii.21). Hence faith remaining fixed in the believer's soul can never be eradicated from it.

In this life however even the believer's faith is never perfected. He is never entirely cured of his distrust and his certainty is always mingled with doubt. Yet we must not on this account assume that faith consists of an obscure and confused understanding of the divine will. The truth is that, in spite of all to the contrary, faith in the believer surmounts every difficulty, and not even partial ignorance or obscure discernment can prevent the clear knowledge of the divine favour. "For as one shut up in a prison, where from a narrow opening he receives the rays of the sun indirectly and in a manner divided, though deprived of a full view of

the sun, has no doubt of the source from which the
light comes, and is benefited by it; so believers, while
bound with the fetters of an earthly body, though
surrounded on all sides with much obscurity, are so far
illumined by any slender light which beams upon them
and displays the divine mercy as to feel secure." (III.
ii. 19).

Also with the years there comes a more stable faith.
As soon as the minutest particle of faith is instilled in
the mind we begin to behold the face of God placid,
serene and propitious; far off indeed but still so distinctly as to assure us that there is no delusion in it.
Then in proportion to the progress we make—and
progress ought to be continuous—we obtain a nearer
and surer view (*idem*). The very nature of the religious
life leads a believer to be a continual seeker after God.
He thus perseveres, and the Holy Spirit is ever with
him to illumine what is dark and lead progressively to
clearer vision. In order to withstand all assaults faith
arms and fortifies itself with the Word of God.

Hope is related to faith as that which expects the
fulfilment. Faith is the firm persuasion of the truth of
God—a persuasion that it can never be false, never
deceive, never be in vain. But those who have received
this persuasion must at the same time expect that God
will perform His promises. Thus faith believes that
God is true, hope expects that in due season He will
manifest His truth. Faith believes He is our Father,
hope expects that He will always act the part of a
Father to us. Faith believes that eternal life has been
given to us, hope expects that it will one day be revealed. Faith is the foundation on which hope rests;
hope nourishes and sustains faith. Hence Paul is able
to say also that we are saved by hope (III.ii.42).

II. REPENTANCE

With faith goes repentance.

This is defined as a real conversion of the life unto God proceeding from sincere and serious fear of God; and consisting in the mortification of our flesh and the quickening of the spirit (III.iii.5). Thus it is regeneration, the aim of which is to form in us anew that image of God which was sullied and all but effaced by the transgression of Adam (III.iii.9).

It will be seen that Calvin here gives a very wide meaning to the term. Even in his own day, as now, there were those who looked upon repentance as but the door into the kingdom, regarding it as that initial sorrow for sin which leads the soul to seek after God, and therefore as the prelude of faith. A man repents and in doing so thereby embraces the Gospel. Those who see it thus are able to draw a clear distinction between repentance and the subsequent renewal of the inner nature by the Holy Spirit (sanctification). Calvin will have nothing of this. On the contrary he insists that repentance follows faith and belongs to it so that the results of faith can be equally regarded as the outcome of repentance. The two cannot be separated except in thought for the purposes of discussion.

Since then repentance springs from faith no man can truly turn from sin unless he already knows that he is of God. Calvin of course will admit that there is such a thing as remorse in the unbelieving heart, and for that matter even a turning from sin, but this is not the repentance which savours of eternal life. This can only spring out of the knowledge of God as redeemer, and until such knowledge dawns upon the soul true repentance is impossible.   Indeed true repentance like faith is the gift of God.

In expounding his definition the Reformer takes up three points.

First, the conversion of the life to God, involves a change of mind and purpose, so that withdrawing from ourselves we turn to God, and laying aside the old mind put on the new.   Thus we require not merely a transformation in external works but in the soul itself. There is no virtue in the external repentance by the observance of ceremonies unless accompanied by the eradication of impiety from the inmost heart and the subsequent study of righteousness.   External acts such as fasting are only valuable to stimulate the inner spirit and call attention to the need for genuine repentance (III.iii.6).

Secondly, repentance springs from a sincere fear of God.   The sinner is first aroused by the thought of the divine judgment, which gives him not a moment's peace, but perpetually urges him to adopt a different plan of life so that he may be able to stand securely at the judgment seat.   To this is added godly sorrow which hates the sin, as well as fears the judgment, because it discerns that the sin is displeasing to God. Further there is a rebellious spirit which must be broken as with hammers (III.iii.7).

In the third place, repentance means the mortification of the flesh and the quickening of the spirit, both of which begin in that union with Christ through the faith which precedes repentance.

In this way again Calvin secures his point that everything to do with man's salvation has its origin in the divine favour and initiative and not in any ability or activity of man.

Mortification is in a sense the destruction of our ordinary nature. We have to renounce ourselves and lay aside our natural disposition. On the point the Reformer writes—" If anyone thinks it absurd thus to condemn all the desires by which man is naturally affected, seeing that they have been implanted by God, the author of nature, we answer, that we by no means condemn those appetites which God so implanted in the mind of man at his first creation, but only the violent lawless movements which war with the order of God. But as in consequence of the corruption of nature all our faculties are so vitiated and corrupted, that a perpetual disorder and excess is apparent in all our actions, and as the appetites cannot be separated from this excess, we maintain that therefore they are vicious; or to give the substance in fewer words, we hold that all human desires are evil, and we charge them with sin not in so far as they are natural, but because they are inordinate, and inordinate because nothing pure and upright can proceed from a corrupt and polluted nature " (III.iii.12).

Hence it is required that we should be ever on the watch lest we be taken unawares in the snares of the flesh. This is the more necessary because the process of sanctification is gradual. The children of God, it is true, are delivered from the bondage of sin but not as if they had already attained full possession of freedom. That indeed is impossible so long as they are in the world. What regeneration actually does is to destroy the dominion of sin by supplying the agency of the Spirit which enables believers to come off victorious from the contest. Sin, however, though it ceases to reign, ceases not to dwell in them (III.iii.11). Thus while the law of sin is abolished in the children of

God, the remains of sin survive to humble them under
a consciousness of their infirmity even though it no
longer has dominion over them.

From all this it follows that repentance is not an
initial act completed once for all at the threshold of the
religious life, as for example in the teaching of the
Anabaptists, but rather a soul-state characteristic of
the Christian to the end. Together with faith it is
indeed the state of mind and heart which in man
corresponds with the permanent self-giving of God in
His free grace. The fruits of it are offices of piety
towards God and love to men, general holiness and
purity of life, in short the whole Christian life of
obedience and service. It is this view of repentance
as a life-long mortification of the flesh, so that the
Spirit of God may gradually obtain dominion over us,
which is the real foundation of the Calvinistic ethics
with its asceticism. And it is not without significance
that actually in the treatment of the subject of
repentance, the mortification of the flesh is given
greater prominence than the renewing activity of the
Holy Spirit.

On this basis the Reformer has no difficulty in
disposing of the doctrine of the Schoolmen and also
of the elaborate machinery of the Roman Catholic
Church. He easily rejects the idea that forgiveness is
dependent on repentance, which the Schoolmen make
to consist of compunction of heart, confession by the
mouth and works of satisfaction. " Contrition they
represent as the first step in obtaining pardon; and
they exact it as due, that is, full and complete "
(III.iv.2). Calvin admits that we are bound strongly
and necessarily to urge every man to lament his sins
and thereby stimulate himself more and more to hate

them. But he contends that when such bitterness of sorrow is demanded as may correspond to the magnitude of the offence and be weighed in the balance with confidence of pardon, tender consciences are sadly perplexed and tormented. Such a doctrine can only drive men to despair. While it is true that forgiveness can never be obtained without repentance it is equally true that repentance is not the ground of forgiveness. The soul must look not to its own compunction or tears, but fix its eyes solely on the mercy of God. Thus Calvin rejects again the notion of salvation by works, even when the word " works " is interpreted to refer primarily to inward motions and dispositions of the soul. Salvation cannot be merited by contrition, nor is it the reward of man's intense desire.

In similar fashion the Reformer rejects the idea of auricular confession as demanded by the Church of Rome while at the same time insisting on the value of confession where it is legitimate. The primary confession is direct to God, because it is He " Who forgives, forgets, and wipes away sins " (III.iv.9). But also one who has so confessed to God will doubtless have a tongue ready to confess whenever there is occasion among men to publish the mercy of God. He will not be satisfied to whisper his secret to one individual alone, but will often and openly in the hearing of the whole world ingeniously make mention both of his own ignominy and of the greatness and glory of the Lord. Hence the secret confession made to God is followed by voluntary confession to men— all for God's glory or in the interest of the sinner's humiliation that he may be edified thereby (III.iv.10).

So at special times of distress, famine, war, etc., a general confession with fasting may be rightly called for, just as in every assembly it is right to begin with the acknowledgment of our unworthiness. Likewise we may for our comfort confess to one another, and the timid soul may seek assurance from his pastor. But all this is voluntary and not to be exacted. The " power of the keys " has place in the Church when the whole Church assembled acknowledges its sins and seeks pardon. Also when one who has become an alien from the Church receives pardon and is restored to fellowship. Again also when the individual seeks and receives assurance from his pastor. But all this is united with the preaching of the Word from which both minister and Church receive their authority (III.iv.14).

The demand for works of satisfaction for sins either before or after baptism, this Calvin decisively rejects. It has no part in repentance because the forgiveness is absolutely free, due to the fact that Christ bare our sins in his body on the tree. This statement as we have already seen is interpreted to mean that as our substitute he endured the penalty and punishment which was due to us. Thus indulgences and purgatory—both modes of supplementing satisfaction —are simply unnecessary and therefore have no place in sound doctrine. So Calvin clears the ground for his doctrine of justification by faith and faith alone.

Chapter V

JUSTIFICATION BY FAITH

I. The Nature of Justification

It may be well at this stage to recapitulate Calvin's sustained argument because the point at which he introduces the doctrine of justification by faith is of some interest. Man needs the saving knowledge of God. This is given in Scripture, Scripture pointing to Christ. Christ is the mediator, divinely appointed, by whom our salvation is wrought. The salvation is apprehended by faith which enables us to get both the requisite knowledge and the assurance. Faith leads to repentance which issues in regeneration. This however is never completed in our earthly life nor can the good works which are the outcome of faith and the evidence of regeneration in any sense commend us to God. We are commended to Him solely by the work of Christ in our behalf. This work of Christ is the one ground of our justification, and so far as we are concerned it is ours by faith and faith alone.

That is to say, Calvin has already defined faith before he comes to deal with justification on the ground of it. Also he has already declared that faith is not without works, though these of course have no " justifying " value. He sums up thus—" Christ, given to us by the kindness of God, is apprehended and possessed by faith, by means of which we obtain in particular a twofold benefit; first, being reconciled by the righteousness of Christ, God becomes instead of a Judge, an indulgent Father; and secondly, being sanctified by His Spirit, we aspire to integrity and purity of life " (III.xi.1). Already the Reformer has dealt with the second of these points, namely sanctification. He now returns to deal with the former. Thus he takes sanctification before justification, reversing the order of experience for the sake of the argument. It gives him the advantage of being able to make clear the precise meaning he wishes to attach to the key-words " faith " and " works " before entering on the controversy in which they play so large a part. Some writers have believed to see in this reversal of the usual order an indication of a stronger emphasis on the idea of Christianity as a life under law than is found in Lutheranism and other types of reformation doctrine.

Justification then is the only possible ground on which salvation can rest and on which true piety towards God can be reared. It consists in the forgiveness of sins and the imputation to us of the righteousness of Christ, whereby we are reconciled to God. That is to say it brings us into God's favour and also makes it possible for the Christian life to begin in us by the activity of the Holy Spirit.

Calvin deduces from Scripture that the term " to be justified in the sight of God " means to be deemed or judged righteous and then accepted on the ground of righteousness. Thus a man might be accepted on the ground of his works if in his life there could be found a purity and holiness which could merit the attestation of righteousness at the throne of God, that is, if by the perfection of his works he could answer and fully satisfy the divine justice. So, in the same way, a man will be justified by faith when, excluded from the righteousness of works, he lays hold of the righteousness of Christ by his faith, and then clothed in this appears in the sight of God no longer as a sinner but as righteous. " Thus we simply interpret justification as the acceptance with which God receives us into His favour as if we were righteous; and we say that this justification consists in the forgiveness of sins and the imputation of the righteousness of Christ " (III.xi.2). This can be only because God has so willed it and made it possible in Christ. So that our salvation depends solely and entirely on His mercy.

The position is that man has no righteousness of his own and no possibility in this life of getting any. But there is a righteousness in Christ made available for him. Such he can receive by faith, and having received it, God then accepts him as righteous, the actual righteousness of Christ being imputed to him in the sense that it counts as his. Thus is God able to forgive and take even sinful man into His favour.

Against Osiander, Calvin strenuously argues that the righteousness which justifies is the righteousness imputed to the sinner and not an " essential righteousness " (III.xi.5). He agrees that justification and sanctification are inseparable, that upon whomsoever God receives into His favour He bestows the Spirit of adoption whose agency forms such an one anew into the divine image. Nevertheless the two things are distinct, and it is important to emphasize that the righteousness which we can plead before God is not our own, nor in any sense the result of our achievement, but the righteousness attained by Christ and freely given to us. This righteousness of Christ is imputed to us while we are still deserving of punishment. Our actual righteousness when it comes is the final outcome of sanctification, and takes its beginning in the justification which is ours through Christ. Hence in a word, our holiness is the result of our salvation and not its cause. We can develop toward it only because God in Christ has already accepted us and in so doing has endowed us with His Holy Spirit. To turn the statement round and say that we can grow in favour with God as we progressively achieve holiness of life is to rob man entirely of salvation and to plunge him into despair.

As is well known this is the point at which the Reformers felt themselves at variance with the Roman Catholic outlook, and believed themselves in their day to be innovators on the basis of re-discovered New Testament truth. And it is here we see most clearly the religious value of the doctrine of justification by faith. It lifts salvation free from the efforts of men, cuts it lose, certainly not from the necessity of obedience, but from its success or failure, and even liberates the sinner from his moods. His ground of salvation is in no sense in himself but in the impregnable rock of God. He fears for his own obedience but he has no doubt of the divine faithfulness. The righteousness is not his but Christ's and he believes that Christ was able to obey. Of the quality of that righteousness there can be no question. Hence salvation is first acceptance with God through Christ, and afterwards obedience and service, and not vice-versa. All the obedience is but the expression of the sinner's appreciation and gratitude. As Paul indicates, it is a question of status before it becomes a matter of service. We are adopted as sons in order to become willing and glad servants.

A splendid example of the way in which the salvation

was viewed in this objective fashion to the profit of a timorous, doubting soul is given by Bunyan. He tells how in a time of fear there fell into his mind the sentence *Thy righteousness is in heaven.* " And methought withal " he writes " I saw with the eyes of my soul Jesus Christ at God's right hand; There, I say, was my righteousness; so that whatever I was, or whatever I was doing, God could not say of me, He wants my righteousness, for that was just before Him. I also saw moreover, that it was not my good frame of heart that made my righteousness better, nor yet my bad frame that made my righteousness worse; for my righteousness was Jesus Christ Himself, *The same yesterday, to-day, and for ever.*"[1]

As we should expect, recalling the controversies of the time, Calvin is rigorous in excluding any possibility of salvation by works, whether those of an external character such as deeds of charity, or those more inward and spiritual such as devotion to God. Not even faith can count as in any sense meriting our salvation. " For in regard to justification faith is merely passive, bringing nothing of our own to procure the favour of God, but receiving from Christ everything that we want " (III.xiii.5). Nor will Calvin admit the possibility of justification by a mixture of faith and works. Some accept the idea of justification by faith but object to that of faith alone. But, argues the Reformer, the one necessarily overthrows the other. Everyone who would obtain the righteousness of Christ must renounce his own so that every ground of boasting is excluded and man's salvation rests entirely on God's mercy. If by works, then the salvation is of debt, but the righteousness of faith is of

[1] *Grace Abounding*, section 229.

grace. Hence even the truly good works which a man
achieves in his regenerate state have nothing whatever
to do with his acceptance before God. Even the
righteousness of the saints is defective and has no
value as a ground of merit.

Any doubt on this point would be entirely removed
by remembering that the measure is God's standard of
righteousness and not ours. With Him nothing can be
accepted that is not entire and absolute and utterly
untainted with impurity. And such has never been,
nor ever will be found in man. Nay, even if one could
by some means satisfy the Law he would still fail
before the tribunal of the eternal Judge (III.xii.1).
Calvin quotes Job to the effect that God could not be
appeased even by the sanctity of the angels (*Job* xv.
15–16). Indeed we have in God a standard of righteousness which is incomprehensible, and yet it is with
this that we have to do. The testimony of men like
Augustine and St. Bernard as well as Scripture proves
the conviction of the human heart that no human
righteousness is enough, and the aroused conscience
is always in the position of finding no other asylum in
which to breathe than trust in the mercy of God
(III.xii.4). This discarding of our own righteousness
is the true Christian humility—" the unfeigned submission of the mind overwhelmed by a serious conviction of its want and misery " (III.xii.6). And this
trust in the mercy of God is the only possible ground
of peace of conscience and a sense of security.

The real place of good works in the Christian
scheme according to Calvin is that by them we
manifest our obedience. They are involved in the
regeneration which is the end of the Christian life,
and on this understanding the Reformer has no

difficulty in insisting on them most strenuously.
Indeed in no system of theology is the demand for
obedience more rigorous. Only, since everything in
our good works which deserves praise is due to the
divine Spirit working in us no particle of it can be
ascribed to ourselves. It is interesting to notice that
in later Calvinism good works came to be regarded as
the evidence of one's election, so that in spite of the
Reformer's own emphasis they came to be highly
valued and to play a large part in the religion.[1]

Lastly this view of justification, it is held, is the
only one which maintains unimpaired the glory of
God. The righteousness of God Himself is displayed
in it, and His righteousness is not sufficiently displayed
unless He alone is held to be righteous and freely
communicates righteousness to the undeserving. For
as long as man has anything however small to say in
his own defence he deducts from the glory of God—
" whoso glories in himself glories against God "
(III.xiii.1). It is worthy of note that the whole subject
is discussed from the point of view of God's righteousness rather than from that of His love. It is God's
righteousness that we need to see and recognize, and
salvation must be ascribed to it and to it alone. So to
ascribe it is to show forth God's glory. The whole
plan of salvation is indeed designed " to the praise of
His glory."

It may be useful at this point to transcribe Calvin's
own summary of his doctrine of salvation given in the
Institutes (III.ii.1).

First, that since God by His law prescribes what we
ought to do, failure in any one respect subjects us to

[1] *v.* Max Weber: *The Protestant Ethic and the Spirit of Capitalism*,
p. 115 f.

the dreadful judgment of eternal death, which it pronounces.

Secondly, because it is not only difficult but altogether beyond our strength and ability to fulfil the demands of the Law, if we look only to ourselves and consider what is due to our merits, no ground of hope remains, but we lie forsaken of God under eternal death.

Thirdly, that there is only one method of deliverance which can rescue us from this miserable calamity, viz., when Christ the Redeemer appears, by whose hand our heavenly Father, out of His infinite goodness and mercy, has been pleased to succour us, if we with true faith embrace His mercy and with firm hope rest in it.

II. CHRISTIAN LIBERTY

After justification by faith Calvin deals with the subject of Christian liberty, which, like Luther, he sees as a natural corollary of the doctrine. The word became a great word in European life after the Reformation period. The idea was first conceived and discussed in connexion with Church rites and ceremonies, but speedily it was extended to the political sphere with far-reaching consequences for the modern world. The Reformers considered it mainly under the influence of biblical texts such as *Stand fast therefore in the liberty wherewith Christ hath made you free.* Calvin maintains it is a matter of necessity since without it the conscience can scarcely attempt anything without hesitation, and justification by faith carries with it this emancipation of the conscience (III.xix.1). The practical necessity of the teaching was in the circumstances of the time. Men had to be emboldened to break with the age-long ceremonies of the Roman Church in order to be able to rest their hope in justification by faith alone. After the lapse of years it is difficult for us to realize the amount of courage required on the part of the average man thus to discard the Roman Church and its elaborate machinery of salvation and embrace with full confidence the simplicity of the Reformation Gospel.

First then, according to Calvin, Christian liberty consists in emancipation from the Law. The Christian must rise above the Law and think no more of obtaining justification by it. As we have seen he still has need of it, but its sole function now is to teach, exhort, and urge toward good. However it is no longer recognized by his conscience before the judgment seat of God (III.xix.2). There the requirements of the Law are not to be considered but only the righteousness of Christ which passes all perfection.

Further Christians now obey the Law not as if compelled by legal necessity, but, being free from the yoke, they voluntarily obey the will of God. In fact it is the liberty itself which leads to the prompt obedience. Thus an element of alertness and cheerfulness is brought into the Christian's obedience such as could not be induced by the severe rigour of the Law. " In a word, those who are bound by the yoke of the Law are like servants who have certain tasks assigned to them daily by their masters. Such servants think that nought has been done and they dare not come into the presence of their masters until the exact amount of labour has been performed. But sons who are treated in a more candid and liberal manner by their parents hesitate not to offer their works that are

F

only begun or half finished, or even with something faulty in them, trusting that their obedience and readiness of mind ' will be accepted, although the performance be less exact than was wished " (III.xix.5). That is to say, and this is the important point, Christian liberty brings an entirely new atmosphere into the Christian life. It supports the new confidence born of the idea of justification by faith and makes a man bold before God and in the service of the kingdom. Nothing truly can be done without a sincere desire to serve the Lord, but this desire can only really flourish where God's favour and willingness to forgive are already known.

Finally Christian liberty means that we are not bound before God to any observance of external things which are in themselves indifferent (adiaphora). Concerning these we are now at full liberty to use or to omit them (III.xix.7).

Without such liberty the Christian conscience is entangled and there is no end of superstition. Questions like the eating of flesh, and free use of dress, holidays and so forth, are now no longer important. " For when once the conscience is entangled in the net it enters a long and inextricable labyrinth from which it is afterwards most difficult to escape. When a man begins to doubt whether it is lawful to use linen sheets, shirts, napkins, and handkerchiefs, he will not long be secure as to hemp, and will at last have doubts as to tow. . . . Should he deem a daintier food unlawful, he will afterward feel uneasy for using loaf-bread and common eatables, because he will think that his body might possibly be supported on a still meaner food. If he hesitates as to a more genial wine, he will scarcely drink the worst with a good conscience; and at last he will not dare to touch water if more than usually sweet and pure. In fine he will come to this that he will deem it criminal to trample on a straw lying in his way " (*idem*).

Hence the Christian is to use the good gifts of God recognizing them as such and giving thanks for them.

It goes without saying however, that he must use all moderately—for life and not for luxury. Some live sumptuously and defend it under the pretext of Christian liberty. They say that these things are indifferent. Yes, says Calvin, provided they are used indifferently (III.xix.9). On occasion liberty consists as much in abstaining as in using (III.xix.10).

This teaching had a very important bearing on the Calvinistic way of life, and shows how the Calvinistic ethic is rooted in the theology. We shall return to it in a later chapter.

A further point with regard to liberty is Paul's view that the use of liberty is to be determined in part by consideration of its effect on our neighbour. It is the duty of the pious to remember that the free power conceded to him in external things is for the purpose of making him readier in all the offices of charity. Hence we are to use our liberty if it tends to the edification of our neighbour but to refrain from using it or to modify it where our neighbour is thereby better served (III.xix.12). So though all things are lawful not all are expedient.

This rule however applies only to things indifferent. Things which are necessary to be done cannot be omitted for fear of giving offence. For as our liberty is to be made subservient to charity, so charity itself must in its turn be made subordinate to purity of faith (III.xix.13). So that while the Reformer does not approve of those who do everything tumultuously and would rather burst through every restraint than proceed step by step, yet neither on the other hand can he agree with those who, while taking the lead in forms of impiety, pretend that they act thus to avoid giving offence. When a neighbour is to be instructed either in doctrine or by example, it may be true that he must at first be fed with milk, but, says Calvin, milk is not poison; and in any case sooner or later he must begin to take meat. So with regard to the changes in Christian outlook and ecclesiastical order, the Reformer puts aside or at least modifies the Pauline point of view. In these matters Christ is obscured or even extinguished unless our consciences maintain their liberty (III.xix.14). From this high vantage ground Christians have fallen if they allow themselves to be bound with the chains of laws and constitutions at the pleasure of men. Even more emphatically he writes " Since by means of this privilege of liberty believers have derived authority from Christ not to entangle themselves by the observance of things in which he wished them to be free, we conclude that their consciences are exempt from all human authority " (III.xix.14).

Not that the Reformer is without consciousness of the practical difficulties of such teaching. He urges that it does not mean that every kind of obedience is thereby abolished. It is clear that he has in mind the revolt taking place in the ecclesiastical world, a revolt which of course he is ready to justify entirely, but at the same time he is not unmindful of the fact that it may be applied in the political sphere. He actually proceeds to discuss this aspect of it, and in doing so falls back rather conveniently on his theory of the two forms of government, the civil and the spiritual. He tries to relate conscience closely to God and spiritual affairs while regarding the civil sphere as to some degree exempt. The civil law binds only the external act and must be obeyed, but it leaves the conscience unbound. The two spheres are to be viewed apart from each other nor must we transfer the doctrine concerning spiritual liberty to civil order. Christians are no less subject to human laws because their consciences are now unbound before God (III.xix.14).

The point is further elaborated in the Reformer's treatment of the relationship of Church and State. In the circumstances it was bound to become one of the most difficult problems for the Reformers. Their theology led inevitably to a new and vitalizing conception of liberty which could obviously have effect far beyond the ecclesiastical realm to which at first they would gladly have confined it. How it worked in Calvinism we shall see later as we trace the development in the various countries. The essential point is that the Reformation doctrine, particularly the emphasis on justification by faith, brought a sense of emancipation to average men and emboldened them to strike out on new lines. Their first essays were in the ecclesiastical sphere, but the spirit once awakened was bound in time to find an application in the wider life.

III. Prayer

We come next to the subject of prayer also connected with the doctrine of justification by faith inasmuch as this opens the way for the right conception of it.

Man, as we have seen, being utterly devoid of the means of procuring his own salvation is bound to seek help from some other quarter. But now having learned through his justification that God is gracious he is emboldened to seek in prayer all those blessings which he has learned are available in God for him. This is what is meant by the Spirit of adoption which, sealing the testimony of the gospel in our hearts, gives us courage to make our requests known to God and enables us to cry *Abba Father*. Thus by prayer we penetrate to those riches which are treasured up for us in our heavenly Father. The eye of faith discovers for us what these treasures are and prayer brings them to us. Hence the necessity and utility of it. We ask both for those things which promote God's glory and also for those that are to our own advantage. Thus the exercise is a normal part of the Christian life. Indeed the sacrifice of praise and thanksgiving can never be interrupted without our incurring guilt, since God never ceases on His part to load us with favours so as to force us to gratitude (III.xx.28).

There is no need to ask why, when God already knows our need and is waiting to be gracious to us, it is still necessary to pray. Those who so argue do not attend to the end for which the Lord taught us to pray. It is not so much for His sake as for ours. Also God wills it. It is the ordained way, and He wills it that due honour may be paid to Him by the acknowledgment that all which we desire and feel to be useful and pray to obtain is derived from Him. It is His pleasure that even those things which flow from His spontaneous liberality should be acknowledged as conceded to our prayers. Thus while it is true that He ever watches over us and sometimes even assists us unasked, yet it is to our interest to be constantly supplicating Him, first, that our heart may always be inflamed with an ardent desire of seeking, loving and serving Him, so that we accustom ourselves to have recourse to Him as an anchor in every necessity; and secondly, that no desire, no longing of which we are ashamed to make Him witness may enter into our minds, . . . and lastly that we may be prepared to receive all these benefits with true gratitude and thanksgiving while our prayers remind us that they all proceed from His hand (III.xx.3).

As to the rules for prayer, the first is that the mind and heart should be as of those who are conscious that they are entering into the presence of God. The mind should be raised above itself, not distracted by wandering thoughts, and free from all levity, which indicates lack of fear. Also we are to ask not indiscriminately but only as God permits. To assist us in this we have the gift of the Holy Spirit who both regulates our affections and determines our prayers. Hence to pray aright is a special gift, an endowment of the Spirit (III.xx.5).

Another rule has to do with sincerity. We must always truly feel our want and be quite sure that we really need the things for which we ask. " So believers ought to be specially on their guard never to appear before God with the intention of presenting a request unless they are under some serious impression and are at the same time desirous to obtain it " (III.xx.6). The repeating of set prayers in a perfunctory fashion from force of habit often with a cold mind and no thought is useless. Repentance is an abiding necessity and it follows that none but sincere worshippers of God can pray aright or be listened to (III.xx.7).

Thirdly, there must be the laying aside of all ideas of worth, a discarding of all self-confidence and a complete submission to and reliance on God. Hence the request for pardon with humble confession of guilt is the preparation and commencement of all right prayer " for God cannot be propitious to any but those whom He pardons." The acceptance of His salvation is a preceding condition (III.xx.9).

Also we should pray in faith, with the sure hope of succeeding, a bold spirit in prayer according well with fear, reverence and anxiety. Nor can we obtain anything without faith since it is faith which brings everything that is granted from God (III.xx.11).

For all prayer Christ is the one and sole mediator. All our intercessions are presented through him, and apart from him there is no way of access to God nor is any prayer agreeable to God which Christ does not sanctify. For those who deviate from this way the shrine presents nothing but wrath, judgment, and terror. It becomes a throne of grace only through the work of Christ. So all appeal to the saints is wrong, and robs Christ of his glory. Also prayers for the dead have no warrant in Scripture. On the other hand there is nothing in the intercession of Christ to prevent the members of the Church offering up prayers for one another though it must be held as a fixed principle that all such intercessions must have reference to the one great intercession (III.xx.19).

Common prayer is valid provided there be no ostentation or catching at human applause, and provided also that there is a true and sincere affection in the heart. For this churches are rightly provided.

Here however we must avoid the old idea that in some special way temples have peculiar sanctity which makes the prayer more holy, or that God is more ready to listen there than in any other place. Also singing is good when it is expressly created to declare the praise of God. We must however beware lest we are more intent on the music than on the spiritual meaning of the words (III.xx.32). Public prayer should always be in the native tongue so as to be understood, the principle being that in all prayer public and private, the tongue without the mind is displeasing to God (III.xx.33). Special times of prayer are recommended for discipline, especially morning and evening prayers and grace before and after meals.

The content of prayer is summed up in the Lord's Prayer. In this Christ has given to us a form in which is set before us, as in a picture, everything which it is lawful to wish, everything which is conducive to our interest, everything which it is necessary to demand (III.xx.34). In his fine exposition of the Lord's Prayer, Calvin finds, first, prayer for all that has to do with the promotion of God's glory; then secondly, request for all that is required to sustain bodily existence; and thirdly, for all that ministers to salvation and the life of the spirit. Thus all things are " summarily comprehended " in this model prayer which our Lord has put on our lips to relieve our minds of all hesitation. No one should wish, expect, or ask anything that is not here summarized. God has taught us what He willed; He willed what was necessary (III.xx.49).

Lastly, before we offer up our petitions for ourselves we ask always that God's will be done. By so doing we place our will in subordination to His, just as if we had laid a curb upon it, that instead of presuming to give a law to God, it may regard Him as the ruler and disposer of all its wishes (III.xx.50). In this spirit we are to pray with perseverance and patience. The life of prayer is our response to God's mercy vouchsafed to us in Christ, and at the same time it is the expression of our desire for complete sanctification in Him.

IV. The Eternal Election

So far in the discussion little has been said to indicate that the mercy of God is not granted freely to all who approach Him in faith, but now the Reformer brings in that severe limitation which for many has seemed the essential characteristic of the Calvinistic theology. " The covenant of life is not preached equally to all, and amongst those to whom it is preached does not always meet with the same reception. This diversity displays the unsearchable depth of the divine judgment, and is without doubt subordinate to God's purpose of eternal election " (III.xxi.1.)

The subject, it is admitted, is attended with considerable perplexity. But Calvin insists that it must be taught. Ignorance of it detracts from the glory of God, impairs true humility, and also robs the believer of the ground of his confidence. Some would say little about it for fear of disturbing the faith of the weak, others allow human curiosity to wander into forbidden paths. Calvin tries to steer a middle course. Where the Word of God teaches a doctrine, he holds, it is sheer perversity on the part of men to keep silent about it. On the other hand let those who talk and write much remember that they are trying to penetrate into the recesses of the divine wisdom and that " it is not right that man should with impunity pry into things which the Lord has been pleased to conceal within Himself, and scan that sublime eternal wisdom which it is His pleasure that we should not apprehend but adore " (*idem*). The Word alone can conduct us to the investigation of whatever is helpful to know and within its boundaries we are confined. Hence we ought to desire no other knowledge of predestination than that which the Scripture reveals, and yet on the other hand we must accept all that the Scripture teaches. The safe rule in learning is to follow where-ever God leads, but also where He makes an end of teaching to cease from wishing to be wise. Thus neither are the secret things of God to be scrutinized nor those which He has revealed to be ignored, lest on the one hand we be charged with curiosity and on the other with ingratitude (III.xxi.3).

Scripture then clearly teaches as follows:—" That God by His eternal and immutable counsel determined once for all those whom it was His pleasure one day to admit to salvation, and those whom on the other hand, it was His pleasure to doom to destruction. We maintain that this counsel, as regards the elect, is founded on His free mercy, without any respect to human worth, while those whom He dooms to destruction are excluded from access to life by a just and blameless but at the same time incomprehensible judgment. In regard to the elect, we regard calling as the evidence of election, and justification as another symbol of its manifestation, until it is fully accomplished by the attainment of glory. But as the Lord seals His elect by calling and justification, so by excluding the reprobate either from the knowledge of His name or the sanctification of His Spirit, He by these marks in a manner discloses the judgment which awaits them " (III.xxi.7).

In elucidating this statement Calvin distinguishes prescience and predestination. When we attribute prescience to God we mean that all things always were and ever continue under His eye; that to His knowledge there is no past or future but all is present; that it is not merely the idea of them that is before Him, but that He truly sees and contemplates them as actually under His immediate inspection. This prescience extends to the whole circuit of the world and to all creatures. It is that attribute of God which makes providence possible. Predestination on the other hand means " The eternal decree of God by which He determined with Himself whatever He wished to happen to every man. All are not created on equal terms, but some are preordained to eternal life, others to eternal damnation; and according as each has been created for one or other of these ends we say that he has been predestinated to life or to death " (III.xxi.5).

Thus predestination is something over and above God's foreknowledge. Nor does the election in any sense rest upon this. God does not fore-ordain to life those whom He foreknows will be worthy of His grace and to death those whom He foreknows will be prone to sin. The election is not in view of anything they possibly will become any more than in view of anything they actually are. It has nothing whatever to do with human worth either possible or actual, but rests solely on the decree. The ultimate is that God has so chosen. As the Reformer puts it—predestination makes a distinction where none existed in respect of merit (III.xxii.6). This is supported by Scripture as, for example, the classic instance of Jacob and Esau. Though brothers, begotten of the same parents, in the same womb at the same time, in all things equal, yet, even before they are born, the judgment of God concerning them is different. He adopts the one and rejects the other. The only right of precedence was that of primogeniture, but even this is disregarded, the younger being preferred to the elder.

It may be interpolated here that in grounding his doctrine of predestination Calvin makes much use of the Old Testament. There we read how God chose a particular nation from among the nations of the earth, and also in that nation He chose whom He would, as for example, Abraham. Always with the covenant idea there goes this principle of selection, and this is carried over to the new dispensation. Here Calvin follows Paul, witness *Romans* ix.–xi.

Then also Calvin is equally emphatic concerning the reprobate. Indeed it is his uncompromising language on this side of the doctrine which has been the rock of offence for so many, and there are still those who would sum up Calvinism in some phrase about the doom of the damned. But the Reformer is merely following through with his logic. If we cannot assign any reason for God bestowing His mercy on His people just as He pleases, so neither can we have any reason for His rejecting others save the divine will. When God is said to visit in mercy or harden whom He will, men are reminded that they are not to seek for any other cause beyond that will. There the finite mind has to leave it.

Calvin with the absolute nature of the will of God in

mind can even go so far as to say that the reprobate are expressly raised up in order that the glory of God may be displayed (III.xxii.11). They suffer nothing which is not accordant with "the most perfect justice" even though we may not be able to understand it (III.xxiv.14).

The Reformer regarded the doctrine of election as essential for the comfort and assurance of believers. The knowledge of themselves as elect is their firm ground of hope. They know it because of their effectual calling in Christ. This effectual calling is the manifestation to themselves of the fact of their election bringing with it in some measure the enjoyment of salvation. When they are called to faith the Father is heard within, and He takes away the stony heart and gives a heart of flesh. Thus He admits them to His family and unites them to Himself that they may be one with Him. The preaching is to all, but the illumination of the Spirit creating faith is only to the elect, God deliberately withholding it from the reprobate (III.xxiv.2). The faith again is the outcome of the election not its cause.

But can the possession of such faith and the other signs of the effectual calling, such for example as perseverance in the Christian way, give the believer a sure and sustained confidence, especially in view of the fact that some seem at one time to be good Christians but later leave the fold and appear reprobate? Calvin here had to face a real practical difficulty. The system tended to make men want assurance since so much seemed to depend on it, and the temptation to enquire for signs is one to which Calvin admits all are prone. But, he urges, it must at all costs be resisted as it can only keep one perpetually miserable. The one thing important is to turn the eyes to Christ (III.xxiv.5). All are elected only in Christ. Consequently we cannot find the secret of our election in ourselves, nor even in God the Father if we look to Him apart from Christ. Hence if we are in communion with Christ we have evidence sufficient. Moreover Christ prays for all his elect that their faith fail not, so that there is no danger of their falling away. The grace of perseverance is not given to all but it is sure to the elect. The following passage on the text *Many are called but few chosen* illustrates the Reformer's point of view—" There are two species of calling; for there is an universal call by which God through the external preaching of the Word invites all men alike, even those for whom He designs the call to be a savour of death. . . . Besides this there is a special call, which for the most part God bestows on believers only, when by the internal illumination of the Spirit He causes the Word preached to take root in their hearts. Sometimes, however, He communicates it also to those whom He enlightens only for a time and whom afterwards in just punishment for their ingratitude, He abandons and smites with greater blindness " (III.xxiv.8).

Here one would think Calvin scarcely avoids the error that he has so vigorously repudiated, namely, that salvation in no way depends on anything within a man or on anything that man can contribute. Else what does he mean by " punishment due to ingratitude "? His doctrine, however, has to face up to the facts of experience and there lies the difficulty. It cannot be said that he gives a perfectly coherent and satisfying account of the matter, and later Calvinists found difficulty just at this point. However, his main

thesis is clear. It is that the election, the only ground
of salvation, depends entirely on the will of God;
that God's will is inscrutable, yet always essentially and
altogether just; and this justice holds as regards the
reprobate as well as the elect. His final word in the
section is—" truly does Augustine maintain that it is
perverse to measure the divine by the standard of
human justice " (III.xxiv.17).

The whole position, as is easily seen, coheres with
the doctrine of God as will and the idea of providence.
It has scandalized, not to say revolted, some, who
have found it so utterly arbitrary and unreasonable.
But it has, perhaps, been made sufficiently clear that
Calvin would not at this point admit the right of
reason at all, both on the ground of its vitiation by the
Fall, and even more because the will of God is absolute
and must of necessity be accepted without question.
Hence when Arminius argues, " God can indeed do
what He will with His own; but He cannot will to do
with His own what He cannot rightfully do, for His
will is circumscribed within the bounds of justice,"[1]
Calvin would have no difficulty in answering him.
There is no standard to which the will of God can
be brought, no justice which is not determined by that
will. That will, indeed, is the one fixed and only standard of justice in the universe. And whatever God wills
is of necessity right just because God is God. So much
surely must be conceded. But then the question is,
can we be sure what the dictates of that will are?
Is Calvin's doctrine of election a right reading of it?
That will, he maintains, so far as salvation is concerned, is revealed in Scripture. Hence it becomes a
question ultimately of the rightness or wrongness of

---

[1] v. A. W. Harrison, *Arminianism*, p. 12.

the Reformer's conception of Scripture and the soundness of his deductions from it. The modern world has moved both from his view of the Bible and from his doctrine of election, at least in the form in which he presents it. The two movements are not unconnected.

One other point is of value for elucidating his main position. He holds strongly that the doctrine of election is absolutely necessary in order to maintain the glory of God. As we have seen, the whole plan of salvation is for the praise of God's glory, and this requires that salvation should be dependent on the divine mercy alone. Now the very fact that the believer's redemption is, in the last analysis, due to the eternal decree, seems to Calvin to safeguard this idea in the most thorough manner. By it the soul of man is brought into relationship with the one great abiding reality, namely the eternal will of God. Dante ends his great poem with the soul of the individual being moved by the Love that moves the sun and the other stars. Calvin puts will in the place of love, but to him also it was a great thought that there is but one ultimate principle in the universe, and that principle both the creator and sustainer of all things and at the same time the saviour and hope of the believer. God is the last word, as God is the beginning, and for Calvin God is active will.

It is strange that this doctrine framed and fashioned for the very purpose of establishing the glory of God, should in course of time have come to be regarded by many as derogatory to the divine character. Many have rejected it or modified Calvin's statement of it in the interests of that very glory which he so strenuously strove to promote. Considering the difficulty of the subject, however, we may perhaps yet say that wisdom is justified of all her children. The names of St. Paul, Augustine and Luther are sufficient reminder that the problem of election and predestination is not one that can be settled by merely being dismissed. It is fundamentally the problem of God.

CHAPTER VI

CHURCH AND SACRAMENTS

I. The Nature of the Church

THE third great section of the *Institutes* deals with the subject of how believers are retained in the fellowship, leading to the consideration of the Church and the sacraments.

Christ becomes ours by faith in the gospel and thus we are made partakers of the salvation and eternal blessedness which are procured for us by him. But because our ignorance and sloth stand in need of external helps, God in accommodation to our infirmity has added such helps and secured the effectual preaching of the gospel by depositing this treasure with His Church. Thus the Church exists that faith may be begotten in us, and may increase and make progress until its consummation. It is conceived as a concession to human weakness, an ordinance of God who has appointed pastors and teachers for the edification and disciplining of his people, giving them authority, and instituting sacraments, which are found by experience to be most useful aids in fostering and confirming faith (IV.i.1). God might have perfected His people in a moment, but instead He chose to bring them to maturity in no other way than by the education of His Church (IV.i.5).

Since then the Church is the ordinance of God no Christian can stand aloof from it. What God has joined let no man put asunder. To those to whom He is Father the Church must also be a mother (IV.i.1),

and since this is God's way of bringing His people to
manhood, all must be under the charge of the Church
till death, " for our weakness does not permit us to
leave school until we have spent our whole lives as
scholars " (IV.i.4). Beyond the pale of the Church no
forgiveness of sins, no salvation can be hoped for
(*Is.* xxxvii. 32, *Joel* ii. 32). Hence the abandonment
of the Church is always fatal. Christianity includes
churchmanship.

Such churchmanship relates both to the Church
visible and to the Church invisible. These the
Reformer carefully distinguishes. According to the
Creed, we are to believe the Church, not *in* the Church.
And this that we are to believe, is not only the Church
as seen on earth, but the whole company of the elect
including those who have died. At no period since the
world began has the Lord been without His Church,
nor shall ever be till the final consummation of all
things (IV.i.17). The true knowledge of this Church
belongs, of course, to God alone, since His secret
election is the foundation of it. Yet with this also
must we be united. Nor is it enough to embrace
the number of the elect in thought and intention
merely. We must think of a unity into which we feel
persuaded that we ourselves are truly engrafted.
For unless we are united with all other members
under Christ our Head no hope of future inheritance
awaits us. Thus the Church is one, and is called
Catholic and Universal, for two or three cannot be
invented without dividing Christ (IV.i.2). This
Church God wondrously preserves while placing it as
it were in concealment.

Since, however, we are not able in this life to
distinguish between the believers and the reprobate,

20562

the Creed means that we are to be in fellowship also with the external visible Church. Since this is, in part, included in the invisible Church, it is equally our duty to identify ourselves with it, and indeed to do so is one of the marks of salvation and an assurance to the believing soul. As long as we continue in the bosom of the Church we are sure that the truth will remain with us. Such is the meaning Calvin attaches to the phrase " communion of saints." Here and now believers are united in brotherly love, and mutually impart their blessings to each other (IV.i.3). Their communion means activity in service, fellowship in the Church below.

To make such fellowship possible God has given us certain marks and symbols by which we may know the visible Church. Calvin describes it as " the whole body of mankind scattered throughout the world, who profess to worship one God and Christ; who by baptism are initiated into the faith, by partaking of the Lord's supper profess unity in true doctrine and charity, agree in holding the Word of the Lord, and observe the ministry which Christ has appointed for the preaching of it " (IV.i.7). Another statement is that " we acknowledge all as members of the Church who by confession of faith, regularity of conduct, and participation in the sacraments unite with us in acknowledging the same God and Christ " (IV.i.8).

The two outstanding marks of the visible Church are thus the Word of God sincerely preached and heard, and the sacraments duly administered and received. These always produce fruit sooner or later, and wherever the preaching is reverently heard and the sacraments not neglected, there the face of the Church appears without deception or ambiguity.

Thus, the Reformer maintains, it is possible for men to recognize and know it.

He is, however, well aware of the fact that the visible Church is by no means perfect. In it there is a large admixture of hypocrites, sinners who are tolerated for a time either because their guilt cannot be legally established, or because due strictness of discipline is not always observed—as Augustine says: " very many sheep without and very many wolves within " (*idem*). Yet in spite of this we are to cultivate the communion. It is vital to our Christian life. Indeed, such value does the Lord set on the communion of His Church, that all who alienate themselves from any Christian society which has the genuine marks, He regards as deserters of religion. Indeed, revolt from the Church is denial of God and Christ, and a " dissent so iniquitous " as to deserve to be crushed by the full thunder of God's anger (IV.i.10).

Any congregation, the Reformer maintains, that holds the order instituted by the Lord in Word and sacrament may be safely honoured as a Church. Nor can it ever be discarded, whatever its faults, provided Word and sacrament are there. Even some defects in Word and sacraments are not sufficient to alienate us from it, still less the unholy lives of some of its members.

On this point Calvin is insistent. All the heads of true doctrine, he says, are not in the same position. Some are necessary to be known so that all may hold them to be fixed and undoubted as the proper essentials of religion, as, for instance, that God is one, that Christ is God and the Son of God, that our salvation depends on the mercy of God alone, and the like. Others again which are the subject of controversy among the Churches, as for instance whether the soul goes immediately to Christ at death, or for a time dwells in an intermediate state—these do not destroy the unity of the faith. Differences of opinion on matters which are not absolutely necessary ought not to be a ground of dissension among Christians (IV.i.12). Also our indulgence ought to extend even further in tolerating imperfection of conduct.

In all this the Reformer is obviously trying to guard against the divisive tendency which the Reformation doctrine produced. He had not, of course, visualized one Church embracing different communities of varied outlook and practice. In spite of such latitude as he allows, he is still under the dominance of the idea of uniformity. It is obvious that he has to find a place in his theory for such differences as existed in the Reformation Church itself, between Lutherans, Zwinglians and his own followers. Hence his attempt to base unity on what he regards as essentials in doctrine. He has no such catholicity as would include Anabaptists, while his attitude to heresy on major points of doctrine is illustrated in the burning of Servetus. Incidentally he seems quite unconscious of the fact that his whole argument could be turned against himself as an arch-rebel against the Church of Rome. The truth is that his doctrine of the Church is still mediaeval. In effect the Church is necessary to salvation, and the old theory of Church membership and its value remains. He is at one with Rome in insisting that the Church is one, that membership in it is essential, that the invisible Church is the true Church. The main divergence of point of view begins when it is asked what are the marks of the visible Church. He has no difficulty in carrying on his controversy with Rome on this basis, viz., that in it, as he holds, neither is the Word preached in its purity and simplicity nor are the sacraments rightly administered. These, the marks of the Reformation Church establish it as the true Church of God on earth.

Here in passing it should be pointed out that Calvin, a pastor all his days, put emphasis on the hearing of the Word as well as on the preaching of it, also on the reception of the sacraments alongside of the right administration. This is a point which has often been overlooked. There is a reciprocal action of minister and people, and in that lies the efficacy of the act, and by it the people of the Lord are edified.

Finally it is in the communion of saints that forgiveness of sins is granted. It is given first at the time we are engrafted into the body of Christ, and then bestowed on us daily, so that we may say that our sins are constantly forgiven by the ministry of the Church, when presbyters or bishops, to whom the office has been committed, confirm pious consciences in the hope of pardon and forgiveness by the promise of the gospel, and that as well in public as in private, as the case requires. This is one of Calvin's interpretations of the " keys " which have been committed to the company of the faithful. Men cannot stand before God without forgiveness, and this benefit is so peculiar to the Church that we cannot enjoy it unless we continue in the Church's communion. Also it is dispensed to us by the ordained ministers and pastors of the Church, either in the preaching of the gospel or the administration of the sacraments. Hence let each seek forgiveness of sins only where the Lord has placed it (IV.i.22).

It will be noted that in all this exposition of the

nature of the Church, while Calvin certainly takes note of the invisible Church, his interest is entirely in the Church visible. He has not that sweep of vision which characterized, say, Dante, nor does he seem to give any permanent significance to the Church triumphant in the life of God. His whole doctrine of the Church is conceived from the point of view of a disciplinary institution belonging to the imperfect life of man on this planet, related closely to man's weakness, and with little or no function once that weakness is overcome. For the mediaeval thinkers the Church is much more definitely the " bride of Christ " with an abiding, eternal value rooted in the necessities of the divine life. Hence with them the " communion of saints " is much more a communion between earth and heaven. Not that Calvin would have repudiated this point of view, but it is not prominent in or particularly relevant to his teaching.

II. PREACHING AND THE SACRAMENTS

For Calvin Scripture is the Word of God and the preaching or proclaiming of it is the ordained method whereby men are to be brought to saving faith. Faith, the great requirement, cometh by hearing. Hence it is by preaching that God brings it forth. So in ancient times meetings were held in the sanctuary " that consent might be nourished by doctrine proceeding from the lips of the priest" (IV.i.5), and just as there the Law itself was not enough but God added priests as its interpreters, so now He would not only have us to be attentive to reading but has appointed ministers to give us their assistance. This by an admirable test proves our obedience, namely, when we listen to his

ministers just as we would to Himself; while on the
other hand He consults our weakness by being pleased
to address us as men, after the manner of men, by
means of interpreters, that He may thus allure us to
Himself instead of driving us away by His thunder
(*idem*). " For who would not dread his present power?
Who would not fall prostrate at the first view of his
great majesty? Who would not be overpowered by
that immeasurable splendour? But when a feeble
man sprung from the dust, speaks in the name of God,
we give the best proof of our piety and obedience, by
listening with docility to His servant, though not in
any respect our superior " (IV.iii.1). A further point
is that nothing could be fitter to cherish mutual
charity than thus to bind men together by this tie,
appointing one of them to teach the others, who are
enjoined to be disciples and receive the common
doctrine from a single mouth.

Hence the Church can be edified only by preaching.
There is no other bond by which the saints can be kept
together than by uniting with one consent to observe
this order which God has appointed in His Church for
learning and making progress (IV. i.5). It is the God-
appointed instrument for both the awakening of faith
in the first instance, and then for the building up of the
people of God in faith, obedience, and charity. Thus it
steps into the place of both the sacramental and
penitential system of the Church of Rome and
becomes the primary activity of the Christian body.
Here again the Reformer has the discipline-idea very
much in mind. To hear the Word continually is a
necessity and a duty. By it progress in the Christian
life is attained. By it God gradually raises his people
to heaven.

Since God then has set such a high value on preaching, He continually raises up men for it. For this express purpose apostles and pastors are appointed, and lest any should think that the doctrine is impaired by the insignificance of the human agents, let it be clear that God so deigns to consecrate the mouths and lips of men to His service as to make His own voice to be heard in them. Thus God Himself is the author of preaching because He connects His Spirit with it and promises a beneficent result. He Himself is the sole edifier of His Church (IV.i.6).

True preaching, however, is severely limited to the Word of God. It is not every utterance even of believing men that carries with it the blessing or has the authority, but only the proclamation of the saving gospel. " Let this then be a sure axiom—that there is no Word of God to which place should be given in the Church save that which is contained first in the Law and the Prophets, and, secondly, in the writings of the Apostles, and that the only one method of teaching in the Church is according to the prescription and rule of His Word " (IV.viii.8). Even the first apostles were restricted in the same way, namely, to expound the ancient Scriptures and show that the things there delivered are fulfilled in Christ. This, however, they could not do unless from the Lord, that is, unless the Spirit of Christ went before them, and in a manner, dictated words to them. They are thus to teach only what He Himself has commanded, and the Spirit is given only to bring to remembrance what His own lips had previously taught. How much more then is the later preacher restricted to the same Word!

Thus we have a static view of revelation. There is the faith once delivered to the saints and now incorporated in the Bible. With that, preaching has to do, and with nothing else. For this reason, says Calvin, the period of the new dispensation is spoken of as the *last times*, that contented with the perfection of Christ's doctrine, we may learn to frame no new doctrine for ourselves or admit any devised by others (IV.viii.7). In fact God deprives man of the power of producing any new doctrine in order that He alone may be our Master in spiritual teaching (IV.viii.9). While the apostles were " sure and authentic amanuenses of the Holy Spirit " so that their writings are to be regarded as the oracles of God, others have no other office than to teach what is delivered in the Holy Scripture (*idem*).

The strength of such a position is seen in such a passage as the following: " Here is the supreme power by which pastors of the Church, by whatever name they are called, should be invested, namely, to dare all boldly for the Word of God, compelling all the virtue, glory, wisdom and rank of the world to yield and obey its majesty; to command all from the highest to the lowest, trusting to its power to build up the house of Christ and overthrow the house of Satan; to feed the sheep and chase away the wolves, to instruct and exhort the docile, to accuse, rebuke, and subdue the rebellious and petulant, to bind and to loose; in fine, if need be to fire and fulminate, but all in the Word of God " (*idem*).

Then allied with preaching are the sacraments. Together with preaching, as we have seen, they constitute that activity of the Spirit of God in the Church by which faith is generated and increased, and the forgiveness of sins assured.

A sacrament is defined as " an external sign, by

which the Lord seals on our consciences his promises
of goodwill towards us, in order to sustain the weakness of our faith, and we in turn testify our piety
towards Him both before Himself and before angels
as well as men " (IV.xiv.1).

Another definition is " a testimony of the divine
favour toward us, confirmed by an external sign, with
a corresponding attestation of our faith toward Him "
(*idem*).

Or with Augustine; " a visible sign of a sacred
thing, or a visible form of an invisible grace."

Here are two things: (i) God's seal and (ii) man's
testimony.

First then, the sacrament is God's seal to confirm
His Word and so to establish us in the faith of it.
Thus with every sacrament there is a promise, the
sacrament being added as a kind of appendix, with a
view to confirming and sealing the promise and giving
a better attestation to it. This promise is the Word,
without which the service is no sacrament at all. The
promise therefore must be proclaimed aloud, preached
by the minister, so that the people may understand
what blessing it is that the sacrament presents
(IV.xiv.4). In this way the sacraments supplement,
as it were, the Word of God, that is the Scripture.
The Lord offers us His mercy and the pledge of His
grace both in the sacred Word and in the sacraments.
Hence Augustine calls a sacrament a " visible word,"
because it represents the promises of God as in a
picture, and places them in our view in a graphic
bodily form (IV.xiv.6). So also they are like pillars,
for just as a building stands and leans on its foundations, and yet is rendered more stable when supported
by pillars, so faith leans on the Word of God as its

proper foundation, and yet when the sacraments are added it leans more firmly as if resting on pillars. Their purpose is thus both to confirm faith and to increase it. They are given us because of our dullness and infirmity. In them God testifies His love and mercy to us more expressly than by word. They are seals of His goodwill, in which, as it were, He adds also His pledge.

Calvin denies that there is any virtue in the sacraments as such, just as a seal on a document is of no value apart from the content of the document. Consequently their efficacy depends entirely on the fact that God has been pleased to attach this value to them, and faith is required to make them operative. Here again the sacraments stand on a level with the Word. In both the Lord offers His mercy, " but it is not apprehended save by those who receive the Word and sacraments with firm faith; in like manner as Christ, though offered and held forth for the salvation of all is not, however, acknowledged and received by all " (IV. xix.7). So Augustine held that the efficacy of the Word is produced in the sacrament not because it is spoken but because it is believed. Another way of stating the same thing is to say that the sacraments duly perform their office only when accompanied by the Spirit, the internal Master, whose energy alone penetrates the heart, stirs up the affections, and procures access for the sacraments into our souls (IV.xiv.9). " For first the Lord teaches and trains us by His Word; next, He confirms us by His sacraments; lastly, He illumines our minds by the light of His Holy Spirit and opens an entrance into our hearts for His Word and sacraments, which would otherwise only strike our ears and fall upon our sight, but by no means affect us inwardly " (IV.xiv.8). Apart from the Spirit's energy the sacraments can avail us no more than the sun shining on the eyeballs of the blind.

Nothing is offered in the sacraments that is not already offered by the Word of God and obtained by true faith. Nor does the assurance of salvation depend on participation in the sacraments. Justification is treasured up in Christ alone and is communicated not less by the preaching of the gospel than by the seal of sacrament, and indeed may be completely enjoyed without this seal (IV.xiv.1). Let it be a fixed point, Calvin writes, that the office of the sacraments differs not from the Word of God, and this is to hold forth and offer Christ to us and in him the treasures of heavenly grace (IV.xiv.17).

All this means, of course, that the sacraments, like the preaching of the Word, can have effect only for the elect. Others may participate, but without deriving any saving benefit therefrom.

Then, in the second place, but very definitely in the second place, the sacraments attest our confession before men. The view that would make them the mere swearing of an oath of allegiance on the part of the believer—the soldier's *sacramentum* to his general—this Calvin rejects. At the same time he allows some meaning to it along with the other idea. " Hence it may be justly said that such sacraments are ceremonies by which God is pleased to train his people, first to excite, cherish and strengthen faith within ; and secondly, to testify our religion to men " (IV.xiv.19). Thus baptism testifies that we are washed and purified, the supper of the eucharist that we are redeemed.

As to the number of the sacraments Calvin allows only these two. These now supersede those given to the Jews in Old Testament times, such as circumcision, sacrifices, etc. In those the Jews received Christ just as we do now in ours, and, to them as to us, sacraments were seals of the divine favour in regard to the hope of eternal salvation. Only now the two present Christ more clearly. Water prefigures ablution, and blood satisfaction. Together they sum up the Christian gospel.

III. Baptism

Baptism is the initiatory sign by which we are admitted to the fellowship of the Church, that, being engrafted into Christ, we may be accounted children of God (IV.xv.1). Another statement is—it is a kind of entrance, and, as it were, initiation into the Church, by which we are ranked among the people of God, a sign of our spiritual regeneration, by which we are again born to be children of God. The end for which it is given is, in accordance with the preceding definition of sacrament, that it may be conducive to our faith and also serve the purpose of a confession before men.

It contributes to our faith three things.

(i). It is a sign of our purification, a kind of sealed instrument by which God assures us that all our sins are deleted, covered, and effaced, that they will never again come into His sight, be mentioned, or imputed. This is the principal thing in baptism. It is not that the water itself possesses any virtue of purifying or regenerating or renewing; still less is it the cause of salvation. Rather the point is that the knowledge and certainty of these gifts are perceived in this sacrament. Our only purification is by means of the sprinkling of the blood of Christ. This the water symbolizes, thus fixing our minds on Christ alone (IV.xv.2).

Nor is baptism in this sense bestowed only for past sin making other sacraments necessary for post-baptismal failures. At whatever time we are baptized, we are washed and purified for the whole of life. Hence as often as we fall in later life we must recall the remembrance of our baptism, and thus fortify our minds so as to feel certain and secure of the remission of sins. In it the purity of Christ is offered to us and is always in force, nor is it destroyed by any stain; it wipes and washes away all our defilements (IV.xv.3).

(ii). Another benefit is that it shows us our mortification in Christ and the new life in him. We are buried with him into death and raised to walk in newness of life (*Roms*. vi. 3, 4). This exhorts us to an imitation of Christ that as Christ died, so we should die to our lust, and as he rose again so we should rise to righteousness. But it goes further and symbolizes that Christ by baptism has made us partakers of his death, engrafting us into it. And as the twig derives substance and nourishment from the root to which it is attached, so those who receive baptism with their faith truly feel the efficacy of Christ's death in the mortification of their flesh, and the efficacy of his resurrection in the quickening of the spirit. Thus we are promised first the free pardon of sins and the imputation of righteousness; and secondly, the grace of the Holy Spirit to form us again to newness of life (IV.xv.5). Both these promises are attached to the ordinance of baptism. The mortification of our flesh is begun in baptism, is prosecuted every day, and will be finished when we depart from this life to go to the Lord (IV.xv.2).

H

(iii). Thirdly, baptism assures us that we are so united with Christ as to be partakers of all his blessings. For he sanctified baptism in his own body that he might have it in common with us as the firmest bond of union and fellowship which he deigned to form with us. Thus all the divine gifts held forth in baptism are found in Christ alone, though implying the grace of the Father as cause, and the sanctification of the Spirit as effect (IV.xv.6).

Such then are the ideas which the Reformer connects with the first sacrament. As against the current opinion of his day he repudiates as false the teaching that in baptism we are set free from original sin and the corruption which was propagated by Adam to all his posterity (IV.xv.10). This corruption never ceases in us but continually produces new fruits, just as a burning furnace perpetually sends forth flame and sparks (IV.xv.2). However, in baptism the believer is assured that the condemnation that original sin deserves is entirely withdrawn from him. It thus symbolizes God's promise that entire remission has been made of both the guilt which was imputed to us and the penalty incurred by the guilt. The sin exists, not so as no longer to trouble us, but no longer to have dominion over us.

The spirit in which we are to receive baptism is all important. Since it is appointed to elevate, nourish, and confirm our faith, we are to receive it as from the hands of its author, being firmly persuaded that it is Himself who speaks to us by means of the sign; that it is Himself who washes and purifies us, and effaces His remembrance of our faults; that it is Himself who makes us partakers of His death, destroys the kingdom of Satan, subdues the power of concupiscence, nay, makes us one with Himself that being clothed with Him we may be accounted children of God (IV.xv.14). Nor does He merely feed our eyes with bare show; He leads us to the actual object and effectually performs what He figures. "Hence from this sacrament, as from all others, we gain nothing except in so far as we receive it in faith. If faith is wanting it will be an evidence of our ingratitude, by which we are proved guilty before God, for not believing the promise there given" (IV.xv.15).

In all this Calvin obviously is visualizing the conscious mind. How then can it apply to infants?

First he deals with those whose baptism was without faith in the beginning, and argues that, though being blind and unbelieving for a long time, we did not hold the promise which was given us in baptism, yet the promise, as it was of God, always remained fixed and firm and true. We acknowledge therefore that at that time baptism profited us nothing, since in us the offered promise, without which baptism is nothing, lay neglected. But later, however, the promise is believed, and so the baptism as it were becomes effective. We reflect thus, he says: God in baptism promises remission of sins and will undoubtedly perform what he has promised to all believers. In regard to us indeed it was long buried on account of unbelief; now therefore let us receive it in faith. Hence rebaptism is unnecessary (IV.xv.17).

This is the argument that really lies at the back of Calvin's attitude to infant baptism and his opposition on the point to the Anabaptists. The baptism becomes effective when the person is able to reflect upon it. He defends infant baptism on the ground that it takes the place in the new covenant which circumcision held in the old. Both rites promised the same thing, namely, regeneration, the only difference being in the outward ceremony. Hence we may conclude " that everything applicable to circumcision applies also to baptism " (IV.xvi.4). So baptism is administered to infants as a thing due to them. If they are partakers of the thing how can they be denied the sign? If the kingdom is theirs why should they not be admitted to baptism, the symbol of our fellowship and communion with Christ? The act of Christ in blessing the children declares both that they are his, and are sanctified by him. How unjust then to drive away those whom Christ himself invites, to spoil those whom he adorns with his gifts, to exclude those whom he spontaneously admits (IV.xvi.7).

How these statements agree with the Reformer's insistence on the necessity of faith, and the understanding of the promise, which, as we have seen, alone makes a sacrament valid, is not stated. Apparently Calvin did not feel the difficulty, though even in his own time there were those who did.

As to the benefits that accrue through infant baptism, it inspires gratitude in the parents as they realize that God extends His mercy not only to them but to their offspring; it inspires the parent to offer the children to the Church, and animates them to surer confidence, " on seeing with the bodily eye the covenant of the Lord engraven on the bodies of their children " (IV.xvi.9).

However, on Calvin's own showing, to be a sacrament it must have effect on the infants themselves as well as on their parents or sponsors. With this question the Reformer actually deals though not without difficulty. His first statement is that children receive some benefit from their baptism, when, being engrafted into the body of the Church, they are made an object of greater interest to the other members (*idem*). Then when grown up they are thereby strongly urged to an earnest desire of serving God, who has received them as sons by the formal symbol of adoption even before they were able to recognize Him as Father (*idem*). This again, however, is a very indirect benefit, and by the opposition which he had to meet, Calvin was driven further.

In order to be saved, he admits, infants must without question be regenerated by the Lord. But how can they be regenerated when not possessing the knowledge of God at all? The answer given is—that the work of God though beyond the reach of our capacity is not therefore null. " We confess indeed that the work of the Lord is the only seed of spiritual regeneration; but we deny the inference that therefore the power of God cannot regenerate infants. That is as possible and easy for Him as it is wondrous and incomprehensible to us. It were dangerous to deny that the Lord is able to furnish them with the knowledge of Himself in any way He pleases " (IV.xvi.18). So again, " those whom the Lord is to illumine with the full brightness of His light, why may He not if He so pleases irradiate at present with some small beam " (IV.xvi.19). To the argument that baptism is a sacrament of penitence and faith which of necessity children cannot possess, Calvin replies by falling back on the analogy of circumcision, but also adds that they are baptized for future repentance and faith—" the seed of both lies hid in them by the secret operation of the Spirit " (IV.xvi.20).

Calvin thus summarizes: " Those who, in adult age,

embrace the faith, having hitherto been aliens from the covenant, are not to receive the sign of baptism without previous faith and repentance; these alone can give them access to the covenant. Whereas children deriving their origin from Christian parents, as they are immediately on their birth received by God as heirs of the covenant are also to be admitted to baptism " (IV.xvi.24).

It certainly looks as though the qualification of birth had here usurped the place of that election of God which is the foundation stone of Calvin's doctrine of salvation, unless we are to say that since the sacrament benefits only the elect, therefore it matters little whether such are baptized as infants or later. That, however, is not Calvin's argument and would indeed nullify a good deal of what he has to say about faith and the understanding of the promise. The truth is that his general definition of sacrament, with its endeavour to steer clear of all magical implications, made it difficult for him to give a logically coherent reason for the baptism of infants. The covenant-idea was obviously responsible for the distinction he makes between the children of believers and others. But then are they in the covenant by reason of their connexion with their parents? Such an idea seems difficult to harmonize with his main teaching concerning salvation.

As to the mode of baptism, Calvin is indifferent save that he prefers the simplicity of apostolic times to the elaboration of the Roman Church. " Spittle and other follies " he repudiates, but whether the person to be baptized is to be immersed, and whether once or thrice, or whether he is only to be sprinkled with water, this is not of the least consequence. Churches should be at liberty to adopt either mode according to the diversity of climates, " although it is evident that the term *baptize* means to immerse, and that this was the form used by the primitive Church " (IV.xv.19).

Lastly it should be noted that the Reformer " explodes the fiction " which consigns all unbaptized infants to eternal death (IV.xvi.26). That disappears before his fundamental position that baptism is not essential to salvation. He thus stands on the side of those who deny the doctrine of baptismal regeneration.

IV. THE LORD'S SUPPER

The Lord's supper is a spiritual feast at which Christ testifies that he is living bread, on which our souls feed for a true and blessed immortality. The signs are bread and wine. These represent the invisible food which we receive from the body and blood of Christ. God like a provident parent continually supplies the food whereby He may sustain and preserve us in the life to which He has begotten us by His Word. Since Christ is the only food of the soul our heavenly Father invites us to him, that refreshed by communion with him, we may ever and anon gather new vigour until we reach the heavenly immortality (IV.xvii.1).

Thus the thing symbolized is the union of Christ with believers. This is made real by being expressed in visible signs showing that our souls are fed by Christ just as the corporeal body is sustained by bread and wine. The end in view in the institution of the sacrament is that we may be " assured that the body

of Christ was once sacrificed for us so that we may now
eat of it, and eating feel within ourselves the efficacy
of that one sacrifice—that his blood was once shed
for us so as to be our perpetual drink" (*idem*).
While we see ourselves made partakers of the body by
eating, we are able to conclude that the virtue of
that death will be efficacious in us.

The supper thus ministers confidence to believers,
assuring them that since they are united with Christ
they are made partakers of all the blessings that come
through him. " Having become himself son of man
he has made us with himself sons of God. By his own
descent to the earth he has prepared our ascent to
heaven. Having received our mortality he has
bestowed on us his immortality. Having undertaken
our weakness he has made us strong in his strength.
Having submitted to our poverty he transferred to us
his riches. Having taken upon himself the burden of
unrighteousness with which we were oppressed he
has clothed us with his righteousness " (IV.xvii.2).
To all these things we have a complete attestation in
this sacrament, enabling us to conclude that they are
as truly exhibited to us, as if Christ were placed in
bodily presence before our view or handled by our
hands (IV.xvii.3).

The chief and almost the whole energy of the
sacrament consists in the words *It is broken for you* ;
it is shed for you. For it would not be of much importance that the body and blood of the Lord are
now distributed, had they not once been set forth for
our redemption. So they are now presented under
bread and wine that we may know that they are our
spiritual food, so that by corporeal things we are
conducted by a kind of analogy to spiritual things. As

bread nourishes our body so the body of Christ is the only food to keep alive the soul. Similarly the wine represents that which fosters, refreshes, strengthens and exhilarates the soul. Thus the sacrament seals the promise of what Christ will be to us, and in doing so it sends us to the cross where that promise was performed and fulfilled in all its parts (IV.xvii.4).

From all this it seems clear that for Calvin union of the believer with Christ is essential for spiritual life. In such union Christ is the nourisher and the believer the nourished. The union is of course spiritual. But then Calvin sees it mainly in terms of the body and blood of Christ. It looks on the face of it as though he substitutes the body and blood, that is, the corporeal part of Christ's personality, for the living spirit. He does this evidently to bring in the actual terms used at the supper, but in so doing he introduces a certain amount of confusion. He seems loath to let go the idea of an actual eating and drinking of the body and blood of Christ. Thus he opposes those who would make us partakers of the spirit of Christ without any reference to the body and blood (IV.xvii.7). Christ's intention, he maintains, was to make his flesh available as our food. " Ever since the fountain of life began to dwell in our nature he no longer lies hid at a distance from us, but exhibits himself openly for our participation. Nay, the very flesh in which he resides he makes vivifying to us, that by partaking of it we may feed for immortality " (IV.xvii.8). By such statements as *I am the bread which came down from heaven* and *The bread which I will give is my flesh*, he declares, not only that he is life, insomuch as he is the eternal Word of God who came down to us from heaven, but by coming down gave vigour to the

flesh which he assumed that a communication of life
to us might thence emanate (*idem*). Thus he is truly
one with us by this our eating of his flesh and drinking
his blood.

It is obvious that Calvin wishes to keep a certain
literal meaning in the terms " body and blood " as in
the terms " eating and drinking." Nor apparently
does he visualize a spiritual union with Christ without
this incorporation in some way in the believer of the
actual physical side of Christ's personality. The
supper means something more for him than a mere
symbol of union. In it he sees also an indication of the
way in which alone that union can be established and
sustained, and, in connexion with this second point,
the eating and drinking of the body and blood have
special significance.

This emerges more clearly still when he asks the
vital question how it is possible for the believer to
eat the flesh and drink the blood. Here he rejects
decisively the doctrine of transubstantiation, whereby
the elements are regarded as being actually changed
into the body and blood of Christ. Also he rejects
Luther's idea of the ubiquity of the body. His own
view is something between. " Though it seems an
incredible thing that the flesh of Christ, while at such
a distance from us in respect of place should be food
to us, let us remember how far the secret virtue of the
Holy Spirit surpasses all our conceptions, and how
foolish it is to wish to measure its immensity by our
feeble capacity. Therefore what our mind does not
comprehend let faith conceive, namely, that the Holy
Spirit unites things separated by space. That sacred
communion of flesh and blood by which Christ trans-
fuses his life into us, just as if it penetrated our bones

and marrow, he testifies and seals in the supper, and
that not by presenting a vain and empty sign, but by
there exerting an efficacy of the Spirit by which he
fulfils what he promises " (IV.xvii.10).

Two principles the Reformer lays down:

(1) Let nothing be derogatory to the heavenly
glory of Christ. This happens when he is brought
under corruptible elements. (2) Let no property be
assigned to his body which is inconsistent with his
human nature—as for example, when it is held that it
can be in two places at once.

" But," he goes on, " when these absurdities are discarded, I willingly admit anything which helps to
express the true and substantial communication of the
body and blood of the Lord, as exhibited to believers
under the sacred symbols of the supper, understanding
that they are received not by the imagination or the
intellect merely, but are enjoyed in reality as the food
of eternal life " (IV.xvii.19). A summary statement
is:—" Christ descends to us as well by the external
symbol as by his spirit, that he may quicken our souls
by the substance of his body and blood " (IV.xvii.24).

From all this it is clear that Calvin is trying to
secure the idea of a real presence of Christ in the
communion service. He will not allow it to become
simply a service of memorial. There must be in it an
actual union of the believer with the Lord, and for
such union the presence of the Lord is as necessary and
must be as real as that of the believer himself. This
apparently he did not see how to secure without
insisting on the reality of the body and blood in some
sense. He could not be satisfied with the spiritual
presence of the Lord only. To one reviewing his theory
as a whole, it seems as though the actual presupposi-

tions of it are no other than those of the old tran-substantiation theory. Though he rejects that view, he is yet not completely emancipated from the thought-forms on which it rests. Anyway he refuses to pass over to that complete separation of the spiritual from the physical which, whether rightly or wrongly, is a characteristic of much modern thinking.

With it all, of course, he makes the same strenuous insistence on faith as with baptism. Christ offers himself to us continually in the supper, but only as we receive him is there any efficacy in the sacrament, and we receive him by faith. But also we are made to feel the efficacy as we actually partake. There must be belief in the heart, but also the appropriation of Christ at the time, our salvation depending not merely on faith in his death and resurrection, but on true communication with him, so that his life passes into us and becomes ours, just as bread when taken for food gives vigour to the body (IV.xvii.5). Here again we have the insistence on the two sides of the relation-ship—God offers, but man must actively receive. Also the Reformer has the note of the unity of the Church symbolized by all partaking of *one* bread (IV.xvii.38).

It goes without saying that Calvin rejected all adoration of the sacrament together with the idea of the Mass (IV.xvii.37). Also he regards it as useless to reserve a portion for the sick on the ground that the hearing of the Word is necessary (IV.xvii.39).

The true consecration is the narration of the promises and the expounding of the mystery, and the service is of value only " to pious worshippers of God." To unbelievers it is turned to the most noxious poison (IV.xvii.40). Our worthiness to receive is a matter of our faith and charity, even though neither is perfect. It is absurd to require for the receiving of the sacrament a standard of perfection which would render it vain and unnecessary, and indeed debar most Christians from participating in it (IV.xvii.41).

As to the form, whether each takes for himself or receives it at the hand of the officiating minister, whether each hands the cup back to the serving deacon or on to his neighbour, whether leavened or unleavened bread be used—all this is of no consequence (IV.xvii.43).

As a typical service of celebration Calvin gives the following :—

Prayer
    Words of institution.
    Explanation of the promises.

The keeping back of those who are debarred by the prohibition of the Lord.

Prayer.

Psalms or other reading while the faithful in order communicate.

After supper an exhortation to sincere faith and charity and Christian obedience.

Thanks to God and Praise.

The atmosphere of celebration is that of Christians frequently calling to mind the sufferings of Christ, thereby sustaining and confirming faith; stirring themselves up to sing the praises of God and proclaim His goodness; cherishing and testifying towards each other that mutual charity, the bond of which is seen in the unity of the body of Christ; and binding themselves to all the offices of love, that none may do anything to offend his brother, or omit anything by which he can assist him when necessity demands and opportunity occurs (IV.xvii.44). The celebrations should be held weekly, as was the custom in the apostolic Church.

PART II

CALVINISM AS AN ECCLESIASTICAL SYSTEM

CHAPTER VII

THE ORGANIZATION AND THE MINISTRY

In the matter of ecclesiastical arrangements the Reformer was faced with two problems, (1) How the Church itself is to be governed and (2) how the Church can play its part in the life of the city or State. The solution which Calvin offered for each of these problems was destined to influence religious life and arrangements in many countries, and from this point of view both the organization and the ideas underlying it have proved to be of great significance. Indeed, A. M. Fairbairn goes so far as to say that Calvin was greater as a legislator than as a theologian, and his polity a more perfect expression of the man than his theology.[1]

Since the Reformation by implication of its theories was bound to dispense with the Roman Catholic hierarchy all the Reformers were faced with the necessity of creating a new church order. In doing so they all looked to the simplicity which prevailed in the Church of New Testament times as against the elaborate organization of the Church of Rome. Calvin himself as usual appeals to Scripture. But it is obvious at a glance that his final system is not just a reproduction of first century conditions. He certainly was influenced by arrangements which he believed to find in the early records of the Church, but it would also seem clear that ideas of government current in contemporary Switzerland played their part, and also

[1] *Cambridge Modern History*, Vol. II, p. 364.

he was influenced, unconsciously, by the example of
sects such as the Anabaptists.[1]   But whatever the
genesis of his ideas, the system proved to be remark-
ably suited to a city like Geneva, and what is more
important, it was found to be capable of being transplanted to other countries, even to those of different
forms of government. This was one of the features of
Calvinism which differentiated it from Lutheranism,
and made it so great a political influence in the century
after Calvin's death.

Needless to say the system of Church government
adopted is closely connected with the fundamental
conception of the Church's nature. The real head of
the Church is not the Pope but God. He alone should
rule in His Church (sometimes Christ is named rather
than God). But as God is not visibly present He uses
men as His substitutes to perform the function of His
ambassadors in the world, to be the interpreters of
His secret will; in short to represent His own person,
doing His own work by their lips, just as an artificer uses
a tool for any purpose (IV.iii.1). Hence in Calvin's
Church the ministry is as important as it is in the
Romanist. It is indeed an ordinance of God, for which
clear reasons can be given. Thus it is the principal bond
by which believers are kept together in one body. The
Lord has committed to it the safety of His Church and
by it Christ dispenses his gifts to the Church and thus
exhibits himself as actually present. Consequently
whoever studies to abolish this order or kind of government, or disparages it as of minor importance, plots
the devastation or rather the ruin and destruction of
the Church (IV.iii.2).

Here is obviously as high a doctrine of the Christian

[1] J. Mackinnon : *Calvin and the Reformation*, p. 80 (n.).

ministry as can be found in Christendom. It is essential to the life of the Church and therefore for salvation. Thus the question of the Church's constitution is a point of doctrine and not merely a matter of expediency. Later Calvinists modified the Reformer's view at this point, but, for Calvin himself, there was one right church-order agreeable to the Word of God, divinely instituted, and that order was vital to the life and continuance of the Christian Body.

By combining the relevant passages in *Ephesians* and *Romans* Calvin arrived at his four classes of office-bearers. *Pastors* who must preach, administer the sacraments, and exercise discipline; *teachers* who are charged with the interpretation of Scripture so that right doctrine may prevail amongst the flock; *elders* who share in the work of government by pronouncing censures and also exercising discipline; and *deacons* who look after the sick and minister to the poor. For the sake of order and peace one pastor is assigned to each church, though he may on occasion assist at other churches. Also in each church there must be a senate with whom is lodged the power of correcting faults.

All the ministers are of necessity ministers of the one holy catholic Church. While Calvin is not unmindful of the needs of the local fellowship, his whole theory of ministry is conceived on the background of the idea of the one Church—the Church of the living God. So in Geneva it was one Church no matter how many churches could be named. Consequently its officers could function as one body. Later the Presbyterian polity evolved a form of conciliar government which enabled the Church as a whole to form and express its mind on any subject under the guidance of the Lord.[1] That development springs straight out of Calvin's theory. He himself refused to grant, in his controversy with Rome, that every council was of necessity a true council of the Church expressing the mind of Christ. He argued that the findings of any such council had to be tested by the Word of God, but all the same he maintained that the officers of the Church (including of course laymen according to his determinations) could, when properly called together in the spirit of Christ, give deliverances for the guidance of the whole body. " There will be much more weight in a decision of this kind, to which the pastors of churches have agreed in common after invoking the Spirit of Christ, than if each adopting it for himself should deliver it to his people, or a few individuals should meet in private and decide " (IV.ix.13). It need hardly be said that this attempt to root the organization in the unity of the Church as a whole is one of the characteristics of Calvinism and had a great effect on later development.

With regard to the authority of ministers to act in the Church this is contained in the fact that they are ordained of God. The ordaining consists of the secret call of God in the heart together with the external call of the Church. Calvin thought of the ministers as exercising apostolic functions and in this sense as true successors of the apostles, but he dispensed with the idea of episcopal ordination. In its place he put this new conception of ordination by God within the Christian Body. A man must first be duly called and then he must answer to his calling, that is, he must undertake the office assigned to him. In the actual appointment Calvin went back to what he believed to

[1] J. Moffatt : *The Presbyterian Churches*, p. 28.

be the practice of the Church of the first three centuries, namely nomination by the bishops and then confirmation by the multitude (so Cyprian). In actual practice, however, the divine vocation was carefully tested. First there was an examination of the candidate by men already in office. This concerned the candidate's knowledge of the Scripture, and his ability to use it for edification; it also included an inquiry into his character and conduct to ascertain if he would be a worthy example as well as a good teacher. After this he was required to preach before the people who were asked to give their judgment concerning him. Lastly, he was solemnly ordained by the laying on of hands, which signified that the Church had made an offering of him to God for the work of the ministry. The laying on of hands is also regarded as a useful symbol for commending the dignity of the ministry to the people. Several hands were laid on but only the hands of pastors already ordained.

In such ways was the ministry carefully guarded, and the immediate effect was to produce a body of earnest and capable men who did yeoman service for the Reformation. But beyond the immediate effect there was the launching forth of this fruitful idea of a trained and tested ministry—a ministry resting on spiritual quality and education, and looking back to God in the last instance for its validity and authority.

Thinking of Calvinism as a whole A. M. Fairbairn writes—" The Reformed minister was essentially a preacher, intellectual, exegetical, argumentative, seriously concerned with the subjects that most appealed to the serious-minded. Modern oratory may be held to begin with him, and indeed to be his creation. He helped to make the vernacular tongues of Western Europe literary. He accustomed the people to hear the gravest and most sacred themes discussed in the language which they knew and the themes ennobled the language, the language was never allowed to degrade the themes. Calvin made Bossuet and Massillon possible."[1] This is high praise. It is in reality a tribute to Calvin's exalted conception of the ministry with its ideal of fitness and training. Incidentally that conception wrought mightily beyond the ecclesiastical organization. When we note that, at a later time, this same combination of the idea of vocation with that of training was applied by laymen to almost every sphere of work in the business world, we lay bare the roots of that individualism which Calvinism everywhere stimulated. In the ministry first, consecration and diligent application were exemplified, to spread later to all departments of secular life.

The function of the ministry is to preside over the Church and train the people in true piety. This involves the preaching of the Word, the administration of the sacraments, and the exercise of discipline. These are divinely appointed functions and constitute therefore the spiritual power and authority of the Church. Since Christ is the head of the Church the minister's chief business is to maintain that authority, and any authority and power conferred by the Holy Spirit on priests, prophets, apostles and their successors is but a delegated authority, and belongs to the office and not to the men themselves. The men, as we have already seen, are but the instruments of the Master.

[1] *Op. cit.* Vol. II, p. 373.

Concerning the preaching of the Word and the administration of the sacraments which is but another form of it, we have already noted the presuppositions of Calvin's theory in a previous chapter. The essential is that for doctrine and preaching the sole authority is the Word of God revealed in the Son and found in the Bible. The Romanists, Calvin maintains, place the authority in the Church alone apart from the Word of God; he, on the contrary, annexes it to the Word and will not allow it to be separated from it. Since Christ rules in his Church by His Word, then let not the Church be wise in herself, nor think anything of herself, but let her consider her wisdom terminated when He ceases to speak (IV.viii.13). So the minister is confined to the Word, and this it is his duty to expound continuously. Everyone knows the prominence given by Calvin to the preaching service.

In line with it is the work of teachers and doctors, whose business it is to give theological instruction together with that preliminary knowledge of languages and other sciences on which such instruction rests. So there arises the need of both a primary and secondary education for the provision of an educated ministry on the one hand and for the training of the young on the other. Since the ideal of education was mainly theological, the professors and teachers also were regarded as being subject to ecclesiastical discipline, and had to be examined and approved by the pastors. Hence the latter became important not merely in the preaching of the Word itself, but in the educational system which was everywhere a characteristic feature of the Calvinistic organization. Educated themselves they were also made responsible for that training and instruction of the people which alone could make their work of preaching possible and effective. It is here we find the link between Calvinism and the later movement toward universal education. The authority is the Word of God. But this idea demands the ability to expound on the part of the minister and likewise the ability to understand and appreciate on the part of the hearer. Hence on both sides education was required. In later times, indeed, not a few illiterate folk set themselves deliberately to triumph over their illiteracy for the express purpose of being able to read the Word of God. Calvin did much to make that accomplishment a necessity in the religious life of men. And he provided for it in specifying the functions of the ministry.

The other task of the ministry is that of maintaining discipline. It is the merit of Calvin (some might rather be inclined to say his reproach) that he tried to make discipline as effective in the Church as the preaching of the Word. His point of view was that, if it is necessary, it must be thorough.

But why is it necessary?

We have seen that Calvin does not take the view of some of the sects, namely that the Church on earth should conist only of righteous people. He admits that the wheat and the tares grow together. However, he maintains that the Church here below exists for the glory of God, and therefore anything that detracts from that glory must be cast out. There must be nothing in the Church to bring disgrace on the sacred name. Also regard must be had to the Lord's Supper which might be prejudiced by a promiscuous admission, " for it is most true, that he who is entrusted with the dispensation of it, if he knowingly and willingly admits any unworthy person whom he ought and is able to repel, is as guilty of sacrilege as if he had cast the Lord's body to dogs " (IV.xii.5). Then also another purpose of discipline is that the good may not be corrupted by constant communication with the wicked.

The authority for such discipline even to the rigour of excommunication, the Reformer believed to find in the New Testament, but here again he was obviously under the influence of the life of his time. Government was required in both Church and State, and the un-settled conditions of the world at the time made a strong government appear the more necessary. Nor could Calvin see how there could be good government in the Church without the power of discipline. " If no society, no house with even a moderate family, can be kept in a right state without discipline, much more necessary is it in the Church, whose state ought to be the best ordered possible. Hence as the saving doctrine of Christ is the saving life of the Church, so discipline is, as it were, its sinews; for to it it is owing that the members of the body adhere together each in his own place " (IV.xii.1). Hence those who argue for the abolition of discipline are seeking the " complete devastation " of the Church. For what will be the result if everyone is allowed to do as he pleases, which must inevitably happen if to the preaching of the gospel are not added private admonition, correction, and similar methods of maintaining doctrine (*idem*)? Thus the idea of discipline springs out of the concep-tion of the Church, which as the body of Christ existing for the glory of God on earth must be a well-ordered, closely-knit body. Discipline is necessary to its spiritual autonomy—a point which Calvin was not likely to overlook.

It should be noticed in passing that it is not primarily from the point of view of the individual Christian that Calvin works out his discipline-idea but rather from that of the Church as an ordered community. It is true that he took sanctification seriously and there are passages where he looks on the discipline as a sort of fatherly correction aiming at the well-being of the sinner. But this does not obscure the fact that the discipline as a whole is not so much to save the soul as to safeguard the Church. If not a perfect Church at least a worthy Church is the Reformer's fixed ambition. In all his thought he has in mind the sad state of the Roman Catholic Church of his own day, notorious for the violations of canon law, and the irregularities which permitted drunkards and gamblers and fornicators to be priests and even boys to be appointed bishops (IV.v.1.) Thus the Calvinistic organization owes not a little to its founder's moral earnestness and his reaction from the laxity of his time.

The specific authority for discipline is found in the power of the keys granted by Christ to the apostles and made permanent in their successors. The Reformer has a twofold idea connected with the keys. The one referred to in *John* xx. 23, and *Matthew* xvi. 19, already noted, has to do with the preaching of the Word and means that the forgiveness of sins proclaimed in the preaching is eternally ratified. The other mentioned in *Matthew* xviii. 18, relates to excommunication, and gives the Church the " word of power " by which it condemns the perverse, and also the word by which it can receive back the penitent. So, says the Reformer, " the Church binds him whom she excommunicates, not by plunging him into eternal ruin and despair, but condemning his life and manners, and admonishing him that, unless he repent, he is condemned. She looses him whom she receives into communion, because she makes him, as it were, a partaker of the unity which she has in Christ Jesus." Moreover, " the Lord testifies that such judgment of the faithful is nothing else than the promulgation of His own sentence and that what they do on earth is ratified in heaven " (IV.xi.2).

This implies a tribunal and a proper judicial procedure. And as the power really belongs to the Word and the ministers are set for the express purpose of preaching the Word, they therefore are particularly concerned with discipline. A lawful consistory, it is maintained, is indicated in *1 Cor.* v. 4, while *1 Tim.* v. 17, mentions two kinds of presbyters, those who perform the office of preaching and those who rule. So in the time of Cyprian it was the bishop in cooperation with the clergy together with the consent of the people (IV.xi.6). Hence Calvin will have such a consistory appointed whose task it is to judge and censure the delinquents. To this he added also the further task of seeking out delinquents, or rather keeping an eye on the flock with a view to being able to report on their conduct.

The forms of discipline are, first, private admonition especially for sins of a private nature, then open admonition and rebuke with excommunication if necessary for sins which cause public scandal. Notorious sinners are to be debarred from the Lord's Table until such time as they give proof of repentance. Thus Calvin linked the spiritual jurisdiction of the Church with the sacrament of the Lord's Supper very much as did the Church of Rome, in spite of the fact that his theological position as against that of Rome made this procedure less strictly logical

In these ways, then, Calvin sought to safeguard the Church and make it the servant of the glory of God on earth. The idea of discipline he shared with his fellow Reformers, but he achieved something new by the rigour with which he applied it. Not all agreed with his strictness. The Zwinglians particularly were suspicious of excommunication, regarding it as savouring too much of the old papal intolerance. However, it was to a large extent by this very power of discipline that Calvin succeeded in making his Church so effective in Geneva, and the spirit of it remained in Calvinism for a long time. Apart from its value to church-life one of its most beneficial effects was that it inculcated a habit of self-discipline in many ordinary men. It thus passed over from an ecclesiastical to a social force.

CHAPTER VIII

CALVINISM ON THE CONTINENT OF EUROPE

I. At Geneva

THE actual organization at Geneva as laid down in the successive editions of the *Ecclesiastical Ordinances* was not at all points strictly in accord with the theory expounded in the *Institutes*. Calvin was not able to get his own way entirely, particularly in the matter of the relation of Church and State. Yet for all that, Geneva gave the first clear indication of how Calvinism would work out in ecclesiastical and civil polity. For this reason the experiment there became of very great importance, and though modifications of it had to be made when the system was transplanted to other countries, yet, by every Calvinistic leader, Geneva was regarded as the pattern which any new organization ought to follow. Since it was an experiment in civil as well as in Church government, it has received a great deal of attention from historians, who have examined it in closest detail and subjected it at points to severe criticism. There is no need for us here to do more than call attention to the outstanding features and indicate their significance.

The aim of the organization was the regulation by the Church of the lives of its own members, and also the attempt to order the whole life of the city. Both these tasks were carried through at Geneva.

In the matter of instruction a valiant attempt was made to ensure that all citizens regularly heard the

Word of God. The city was divided into three
parishes, St. Peter's, St. Gervais, and the Madeleine.
Five ministers were appointed with three assistants.
These together with pastors from the surrounding
country held weekly conferences for mutual instruction and encouragement. Arrangements were fixed for
preaching services on Sundays, two at daybreak,
others in each of the three churches at nine o'clock,
catechism for the young at noon, and sermons again
in all parishes in the afternoon. Also preaching
services on Mondays, Wednesdays and Fridays—as
Mackinnon adds, seventeen sermons per week in a
town of about 13,000 inhabitants.[1] Communion was
held quarterly, and also public lectures on occasion.
Attendance at divine worship was enforced with fines
as penalties for absence and watchmen were appointed
to catch delinquents. The underlying idea in it all
was instruction in the theology, though of course the
thought of worship was not altogether absent.

Then at the back of all this preaching activity was
the carefully planned educational system. The
children were taught their catechism and instructed
in the church, and when Calvin finally achieved his
ambition there was the school and the university.
The school or college offered a graduated course in
preparation for the more advanced studies. The
curriculum comprised mainly the Latin and Greek
classics, with, later, the study of logic, rhetoric, and
exercises in style and declamation. The New Testament in Greek was read weekly. Prizes were given by
the City Council, and the prize-giving was held in the
Church of St. Peter's. A large place, of course, was
allotted to religious exercises—morning instruction

[1] *Calvin and the Reformation*, p. 78.

with the Lord's Prayer, an hour at Psalm-singing daily, repetition of the Creed and the Ten Commandments. Also the students attended the two sermons on Sundays, and the one on Wednesdays, and also the Sunday catechism. Each quarter before the communion service one of the ministers addressed the whole school on the subject.

The higher department of the educational system, the academy, was under the Rector who actually had charge of all the education in the city. Under him there were professors of Greek, Hebrew, the arts, and two of theology. Twenty-seven lectures were given each week. A weekly discussion presided over by one of the pastors, and a monthly disputation on some theological theme, fitted those who desired to equip themselves for the exposition of the Scriptures. All the professors from the Rector downwards and all the students had to subscribe to the Calvinistic standard of doctrine, which naturally limited and crippled the education given. However, in spite of its manifest defects it was nevertheless the launching of a great idea. " Calvin believed," writes A. M. Fairbairn, " in the unity of knowledge and the community of learning, placing the magistrate and the minister, the citizen and the pastor, in the hands of the same teacher, and binding the school and university together. The boy learned in the one and the men in the other; but the school was the way to the university, the university was the goal of the school."[1] We have already noticed the same writer's tribute to the character of the Reformed ministers indicating the kind of fruit the system produced in the wider fields of Calvinism, and there is abundant testimony to its

[1] *Cambridge Modern History*, Vol. II, p. 372.

effectiveness in the city itself. It created a culture, narrow truly when judged by modern standards, but nevertheless firmly based on the new learning of the time and braced by the mental discipline of a constant pre-occupation with the great themes of theology.

The second instrument, namely the persistent application of discipline, led to that regimentation of the city's life which has appeared to later generations almost fantastic. For both Church and State it was regarded as essential for good order, and to be enforced at all costs. Nor were any, either clergy or laity, either rich or poor, exempt from it. There is thus much indeed to be said for it, it knew no respect of persons. Indeed some of Calvin's sternest battles were fought against the well-to-do to vindicate this very point. His sentiment was well expressed by his own quotation of Chrysostom—" Let us not be afraid of sceptres or diadems or imperial robes, we have here a greater power." Thus if there was a spirit of rigour there was also a rigorous and even justice, and this not only with reference to offences against the Church, but equally with offences of a more private nature. All without exception were to be brought under a uniform standard.

It began with the pastors themselves. We have seen that they have to be men of character as well as good teachers. Throughout their period of ministry they are answerable to the higher authority. Such sins as heresy, schism, violation of ecclesiastical law, blasphemy, impurity, perjury, avarice, usury, dancing and so forth are not to be tolerated. It is quite in the spirit of Calvinism that the list also included negligence in the study of the Scriptures. At their regular weekly meetings the pastors were encouraged to criticize one another's conduct, including both study and pastoral visitation, as well as moral faults, and in this task the youngest had the same privilege as the oldest. Indeed such criticism was laid on the conscience of each as a solemn duty, each being made responsible for the right conduct of his brethren. However, it would be a mistake to assume that the meeting was a time of carping criticism. Its purpose was edification and encouragement in the work, and there is no doubt that this serious purpose was in the main achieved.

For the Church, elders were appointed to act with the pastors. These made a yearly visitation of every member of the Church to test both conduct and doctrine. This arrangement gave the laity also a place in the exercise of discipline.

Further, the elders with the pastors formed the Consistory, which met weekly to receive and examine reports concerning any irregularities of conduct. This Consistory could inflict any spiritual punishment even to exclusion from the Lord's table. Also it could, when necessary, hand over offenders to the civil authority to be punished according to the civil law.

The civil government was the Council of the City, which, probably contrary to Calvin's own wish, had more influence in the affairs of the Church than was wise. It chose the pastors, though with a right of veto reserved to the Church, elected the elders from its own body, and also appointed the deacons. In actual practice the personnel of the Council was much the same as that of the Consistory. This led to confusion between the civil and the ecclesiastical government and tended to confuse the offences that belonged to the one sphere with those of the other. Thus it

K

perpetuated what Mackinnon calls " the vicious mediaeval idea "[1] of punishing spiritual offences with civil penalties.

That the régime was tyrannical, at least from the point of view of the modern mind, would be readily conceded. One has only to cast the eye even casually over the list of punishable offences and the fines attached to each to see that the standard was absurdly different from our own. We read with amused surprise that every citizen had to be indoors by nine o'clock, and that even the number of dishes at meals was regulated; with less surprise perhaps that all noisy games, all games of chance, and dancing and the singing of profane songs, together with drunkenness, immorality, extravagance and immodesty in dress were forbidden. The savage sentences inflicted even on children for trivial offences reminds us of our own eighteenth century; the ban on theatres, novel reading and the like of the early Puritans.[2] It is pointed out by the defenders of Calvin that most of this legislation was in accord with the tradition of a mediaeval city like Geneva. All the Reformer did, it is claimed, was to enforce laws already existing. This certainly is true, and the mere mention of eighteenth-century conditions in our own land is sufficient to remind us that not all the barbarity in European legislature can be laid at the door of the new religion. Still the fact remains that the Reformer gladly accepted the old system and used it vigorously for his new purpose. Also it must be admitted that much of the legislation was in line with his theological

---

[1] Mackinnon: *Op. cit.* p. 82.

[2] For details of offences and fines see Schaff: *History of the Church*: *Swiss Reformation*, Vol. II, p. 489 ff.

outlook, and, in that sense at least, belongs to Calvinism in its first phase. Also the spirit of the system as
applied at Geneva, quite apart from the details of the
legislation, is essentially Calvinistic, as is shown by
the fact that the same type of legalism re-appeared in
every country which Calvinism at a later date
dominated.

However, we must not be led astray by this modern
feeling concerning the so-called tyrannical element.
We shall misconceive the spirit of Geneva altogether
if we take account only of the recalcitrant element
which naturally looms large in the records just because
it was recalcitrant. The majority of the citizens
were firmly with Calvin. Many were truly filled with
an ardent desire to live a worthy life, and were ready
to accept rebuke and acknowledge their faults. The
discipline was by no means resented to the extent
which the modern mind is apt to assume. It was in
line with religious tradition, and the capacity for
accepting admonition was much greater then than it
is to-day. Nor must we forget that in the city there
existed all the moral earnestness and spiritual power
of a genuine revival. The immediate outcome of the
régime was far more prominent in the minds of the
best men of the day than were any reflections concerning the hardship of it. It certainly cleaned up one
of the most immoral cities of the age. The victory
over the libertines and other disorderly groups was
complete and decisive. To us it may seem that the
restriction of individual liberty went beyond all
reasonable limits, but to the Reformers themselves, the
experiment was a conspicuous success, to some of
them, indeed, the most conspicuous in Europe. Calvin,
it must be admitted, did achieve a city-state on a new

model in which religion and discipline undoubtedly
brought life to power. The city won a great place in
the affairs of Europe and an honourable prestige, so
that, provided one accepted the position, one could be
inordinately proud of being a citizen of it. Students
from all parts flocked to its university and most of the
Reformation leaders of the second generation were
drawn into its orbit. The testimonies which some of
them have put on record show a spirit of genuine
enthusiasm. Farel declared he would rather be the
last in Geneva than the first anywhere else. John
Knox called it the most perfect school of Christ that
ever was in the earth since the days of the Apostles,
while Valentine Andreæ, a Lutheran, speaking of the
city as he found it in 1610, nearly fifty years after
Calvin's death says—" I observed something great
which I shall remember and desire as long as I live.
. . . What a glorious ornament of the Christian
religion is such a purity of morals! " He goes on to
lament that the same is not found in his own Church
and country.[1] Nor did this pleasing condition of the
city's life speedily pass away. It is indeed true to
say that Calvin's rule laid the foundation of both the
spiritual and material prosperity of the city of his
adoption. It has never looked back, and it is fitting
that to-day his monument is within its walls.

In this connexion it should be noticed in passing
that if his régime was strict he did not a little to make
it possible. One writer says that sanitation is a
distinctly Protestant contribution to European civilization.[2] In saying it he may well have Calvin in

[1] Schaff: *op. cit.* Vol. II, p. 518, where the full quotations are
given.
    David Ogg: *The Reformation* (Benn's Sixpenny Library), p. 71.

mind, for the Reformer laboured for a clean, healthy and prosperous city, and Geneva, amongst its other merits, offers us the sight of a serious attempt on the part of earnest Christian men to tackle civic and social problems. Thus the Reformer insisted on the removal of filth from houses and streets, and provided for the supervision of the markets to prevent the sale of uneatable food. Low taverns and drinking shops were abolished, and street begging restricted. On the positive side, a hospital and a poor-house were established, and efforts made to find work for the unemployed. Calvin himself was the originator of the scheme whereby the silk industry was started in the city. He both worked out the detailed plan and induced the treasury to provide the money. Factories were built and the industry greatly flourished.[1]

Thus, taking it as a whole, we have ocular demonstration of the ability of the Church, when it is so determined, to order the life of the whole community. Nor was this success ever forgotten by Calvinism. Geneva gave the idea and also the proof of the idea's practical value. It sent men out to other countries with both the desire to re-order the life of the State and with detailed knowledge of the kind of organization and practical schemes required for doing it. This ideal has wrought in the minds of Calvinists even on to the present time. The Church is in no sense a little garden walled round. On the contrary, it has a solemn responsibility for the life of the city or nation. Public morality and general living are its care. If the Church is the centre the confines of its influence are the boundaries of the State. Its aim is to create a real community life. It is that river, the streams

[1] v. Schaff: *op. cit.* pp. 516-7.

whereof make glad the city of God. If there have
been in history two illustrations of the Church
dominating the world, the one, on the grand scale,
was that of the Catholic Church in the Middle Ages,
the other that of the theocracy at Geneva.

II. The Reformed Church in Switzerland, Germany and the Netherlands

We now turn to note the fate of Calvinism in
Europe and America, a survey necessarily brief, but
nevertheless giving some indication of its wide dis-
semination and its enormous influence in the life of
the world.

In Switzerland itself the Reformation had been
started by Zwingli and his influence undoubtedly
remained. But it was inevitable if only by reason of
geographical situation that Geneva should make
itself felt. While the Church continued to retain the
essentially democratic character which Zwingli had
impressed upon it, both its doctrinal statements and
its organization soon began to show the influence of
Calvinism. Calvin himself was in close touch with the
whole movement during his lifetime and it was
owing largely to his personal influence that the
theological differences in the country were reconciled
and one type of doctrine spread through all the
Reformed Churches. Bullinger, the successor of
Zwingli, accepted Calvin's views on the Lord's Supper
in 1549 and three years later the *Consensus Genevensis*
made the doctrine of predestination official. Then
after Calvin's death most of the pastors remained
under Genevan influence, Beza holding an acknowledged authority throughout the whole country.

Calvin's *Catechism for Children* was widely used and the *Zurich Confession* was put out as the authoritative statement on the doctrine of the sacraments. The *Second Helvetic Confession* published in 1566 in the name of all the Swiss cantons except Basel and Neufchâtel, is one of the fullest expressions of unadulterated Calvinism, and as such enjoyed wide popularity.

In a similar manner the spirit of Calvin permeated the Rhine region of Germany—that region which was so greatly disturbed first by the Peasants' revolt and then by the Anabaptists. It is generally agreed that the revolt lost Luther the peasant class in this area. But where Lutheranism failed, while many of the disillusioned peasants became Anabaptists, the better class who were so minded turned to Calvinism. The Genevan model appealed particularly to the free cities, four of which—Strasburg, Constance, Memmingen and Lindau had already presented to the Diet of Augsburg (1530) the Confession known as the *Tetrapolitan* refusing communion with the Lutherans. The influence of Strasburg, where it will be remembered Calvin himself had laboured for a time, was particularly important.

Then Calvinism also gained ascendancy in the Palatinate under the Elector Frederick III. His successor Louis VI took the province back to Lutherism for the years 1576–83, but it returned again to Calvinism under Frederick IV. Under the third Frederick the famous university of Heidelberg became a great centre of Calvinism, and, at the instance of the Elector, the *Heidelberg Catechism* was drawn up, largely the work of Ursinus, a pupil of Melanchthon, and Olevianus, a pupil of Calvin. This statement owed

much to Calvin's *Catechism for Children* and gained
wide popularity, becoming the creed of the Reformed
Churches of Germany. Brandenburg also became a
province of Calvinism until the union of the Lutheran
and Reformed Churches of Germany in 1817. Other
provinces of Germany that were Calvinistic for a time
were Anhalt-Nassau, Hesse-Cassel, and Bremen. Also
not a few of the later Lutheran statements of faith
show an infiltration of Calvinistic doctrine. It is
interesting to note that Poland, Bohemia, Moravia
and Hungary were all influenced by it.

In the Netherlands the Church became thoroughly
Calvinistic under the duress of persecution. Here the
religion played its part in the successful rising against
Philip II and the Duke of Alva, which resulted in the
independence of the seven provinces under the leader-
ship of William of Orange. Thus Calvinism came to be
linked in the Dutch mind with national aspiration and
independence. At the commencement of the trial
almost all sections of the Reformation movement were
represented in the Netherlands, but in 1569 at a
meeting at Emden it was resolved that the Church
should be ruled by consistories, classes and synods.
That is to say the Presbyterian form of government
was adopted. As Lindsay says—" The consistorial
system of the Lutheran Church and the position
which Zwingli assigned to the magistracy are possible
only when the civil government is favourably disposed
towards the Church within the land which it rules; but
Presbyterianism, as France, Scotland, and the Netherlands have proved, is the best suited for ' a Church
under the cross.' "[1] William of Orange declared himself
a Calvinist in 1573. However, since the seven

[1] T. M. Lindsay: *History of the Reformation*, Vol. II, p. 271.

provinces were not united as a single nation, each had its own organized Church, and only with difficulty could they meet together as one united body.

The Dutch confession of faith known as the *Belgic Confession* was Calvinistic, based on that of the French Protestant Church. It was revised by Francis Junius, a disciple of Calvin, in 1561 and approved at Dortrecht in 1572. This became the confession of all the Churches and made Calvinism the creed of Netherland Protestantism. The Churches also adopted the *Heidelberg Catechism* for the training of the young.

One of the results of the winning of independence on the part of the seven provinces was the growth of the universities—quite in the spirit of Calvinism. The university of Leyden was founded in 1575 as an offering of gratitude for the deliverance of the city from the siege, and quickly became famous as a centre of Calvinism. Franecker, Groningen, Utrecht and Harderwyk followed soon after. These all became schools of theological training and attracted students from many countries. By the seventeenth century the Dutch theologians had won a place and reputation throughout the Christian world. Their influence on Protestantism generally was very great and accounted for the further spread of Calvinism.

However, we must notice that it was in Holland that the first effective check to Calvinistic doctrine arose. From the very beginning there had been those who opposed the rigour of the doctrine of predestination, and further reaction to it was stimulated by the extreme lengths to which some of its advocates carried their views. This resulted ultimately in the teaching of Arminius and the Remonstrants, giving rise to what is known as Arminianism. The controversy was carried on with vigour not to say bitterness. Holland became the first battle-ground of a controversy that was to last for more than a century. At the Synod of Dort in 1619 Arminianism was condemned, and the *Belgic Confession*, somewhat revised, accepted as the doctrinal basis of the Dutch Church. The revised form of the Confession " adopted the five knotty canons of unconditional predestination, limited atonement, total depravity, irresistible grace and the perseverance of saints."[1] However, Arminianism still continued to flourish and ultimately influenced the whole Church.[2]

Lastly, before leaving Holland, we recall that the country became for a time the centre of the Covenant type of Reformation doctrine. Anabaptism continued to flourish amongst a section of the population, leading to the Church of the Mennonites and also to types of independency. From these groups later emerged the Pilgrim Fathers, who, as we shall see, also came under the influence of Calvinism and thus took the spirit and discipline to the New World. Also from the same groups came influences affecting the religious life of England. In these ways Holland became an important radiating centre of Reformation doctrine, and particularly of the Calvinistic type. Its natural expansion and commercial success in the succeeding century added greatly to its influence.

III. CALVINISM IN FRANCE

In France the fate of Calvinism was very different—success, struggle and eclipse.

[1] Schaff: *op. cit.* Vol. II, p. 815.
[2] *v.* A. W. Harrison: *Arminianism* (Duckworth's Theology Series).

We begin by noting that the Reformer himself was a Frenchman, and it is perhaps not unreasonable to seek the very origins of Calvinism in the early French Protestant Church, seeing it was there that Calvin was converted to the Reformation doctrine. His early contacts are well known. Pierre Robert Olivétan, the translator of the Bible into French (Calvin himself had a hand in it) was his cousin, and, like himself, a native of Noyon. Other contacts were made during student days, notably that with the group of Meaux, of which group Farel, who later brought Calvin to Geneva, was also a member. His conversion, which probably took place at Orleans, led him to throw in his lot with the evangelicals of Paris from which time he went forward in his reforming work without looking back. Certain it is that he never lost his sense of nationality, and though his work was organized just over the border—in a way which would not have been allowed in France itself— yet it was in his own mind an organization for his native country as well as for Geneva. As a matter of history, during his whole life-time Calvin was the real head of the Reformation in France. It was because of the persecution in France that the *Institutes* was conceived and written, being in the first edition addressed to the French king, Francis I, and translated immediately after its publication into French,— as the writer said, for the use of his own countrymen.

So in due time almost all the leaders of the Reformation in France were Geneva-trained. It is a known fact that within the eleven years 1555 to 1566 the city sent no less than a hundred and sixty-one pastors into France. Most of these were travelling evangelists covering a wide area and spreading the new gospel

among the masses of the people. During the period
of the persecution many ardent young men came as
refugees to the Swiss city, there to be instructed by
Calvin that they might return again to France carrying tracts and books proclaiming the reformed
doctrine. The training of such collaborators was a
very congenial task to the Reformer.

As to the development of the cause in France it is
hardly necessary to repeat the story of the splendid
martyrdom of the Huguenot Church in its long
struggle against both the absolutism of the monarch
and the hostility of the Roman Church. The courage
with which its devotees faced death for the sake of the
Gospel is one of the epics of Protestantism, and as
such is well known. Here we need merely emphasize
the fact that it was Calvinism which nerved them for
high endeavour, which indeed both set the enterprise
and sustained them in it. It was the same spirit
drawn from the same source which inspired William
of Orange and his co-religionists, John Knox and the
Covenanters, in some measure Oliver Cromwell and
the Roundheads, and the Pilgrim Fathers. An outstanding feature of Calvinism, as almost every writer
on the subject has noticed, was this remarkable power
it possessed of infusing courage and a spirit of activity
into ordinary men. In France its symbols were the
bush that burned but was not consumed, and the
anvil smitten but not broken.

That it was Calvinism in France is clear from the
nature of the organization. Indeed it is claimed that
Calvinism as an ecclesiastical system was more fully
and logically wrought out in France than even at
Geneva, where, as we have seen, a measure of compromise was inevitable. At first local congregations

organized themselves on the Genevan model under pastors trained at Geneva, then in 1559 the first national synod was held. Here the *Confessio Gallica* was drawn up, based on a short confession composed by Calvin. This became the Confession of the French Protestant Church and is one of the classic expressions of Calvinism. Also the *Book of Ecclesiastical Discipline* was issued, modelled on Calvin's *Ordinances* though with some differences. Here the system was thoroughly representative, not to say democratic. The consistories already appointed in several churches were recognized, elders and deacons were to be re-elected annually. Provincial synods were established to meet twice a year as courts of appeal, each congregation sending its pastor and one elder. Then the whole Church was united under the national synod or General Assembly, which became the ultimate ecclesiastical authority. " It is interesting," writes Lindsay, " to see how in the midst of a country whose government was yearly becoming more arbitrary and absolutist, this ' Church under the cross ' organized for itself a government which reconciled more perfectly, perhaps, than has ever been done since, the two principles of popular right and supreme central control."[1]

The Church continued to hold national synods till 1660 when they were prohibited by Louis XIV. In 1685 came the revocation of the Edict of Nantes, and the next synod, the thirtieth, was not held till 1872. The devastating effect of the revocation of the Edict of Nantes, driving many Huguenots overseas and severely restricting Protestant activities in France,

[1] T. M. Lindsay: *The Reformation* (Handbooks for Bible Classes), p. 79.

brought to a close one of the most heroic struggles
that religion has ever inspired. It has to be registered
as a defeat for Calvinism, though the Protestant
Church in France is still alive, and the struggle was
not without its effect on French national character
and life. It paved the way to some extent for the
reception of the democratic idea in France, when that
idea, fostered in the Calvinism in America, returned
across the Atlantic to fire the imagination of oppressed
masses reaching out to revolution against the very
monarchism that Calvinism had previously chal-
lenged. A survey of world history makes clear a
connexion between Calvin and the Revolution,
though, needless to say, the Revolution itself would
have been anathema to his conservative mind. The
Huguenot struggle thus has its place in the story of
man's march to freedom. The trek of the Huguenots
both east and west also added to their service in the
spread of Calvinism.

A note here may be added concerning the Waldenses
who also became Calvinistic and shared the persecution. They were a people who from their origin in
mediaeval times had based their life on the Bible and
followed apostolic simplicity. When the Reformation
began, recognizing that it was of the same spirit and
intention as themselves, they made inquiries of its
leaders and ultimately threw in their lot with the new
movement. They lived in the Alps, many in Pied-
mont, others in Provence. Farel with other reformers
met a section of them at a conference at Chamforans
in 1532. This led to the drawing together of the
Waldenses with the Swiss Reformation and subse-
quently to their adoption of Calvinism. Incidentally
it was this conference that inspired Olivétan to make

his French translation of the Scriptures. The section of them living in Provence was bitterly persecuted in the reign of Francis I, 1545, when their chief towns, Merindol and Cabrières, together with twenty-eight villages, were destroyed and four thousand persons slaughtered. During the successive persecutions great numbers of them sought refuge in flight, and as many as four thousand went to Geneva where Calvin opened a subscription list for them, and where many of their future pastors for all districts were afterwards trained. The *Waldensian Confession* of 1655 is Calvinistic, based on the *Gallican Confession* of 1559. After further persecution, notably that under Louis XIV against which Cromwell protested and Milton wrote his famous sonnet :

> Avenge, O Lord, thy slaughtered saints, whose bones
> Lie scattered on the Alpine mountains cold ;

the Waldenses obtained freedom in 1848, since which time they have been zealous evangelists in Italy.

It is interesting to note that a section of them from Bohemia sent a deputation to Calvin at Strasburg in 1540. These ultimately went to Poland. Calvin wrote commending them to the Reformed Churches of that region.

Chapter IX

CALVINISM IN THE ENGLISH-SPEAKING
WORLD

I. Presbyterianism in Scotland

A FULL account of Calvinism in Scotland would involve a complete history of the Reformation in that country. Nowhere did the spirit of Calvin more thoroughly permeate the national life, and the present Church of Scotland may well be regarded as the purest lineal descendant of Geneva in existence.

This was mainly due to John Knox. The earlier reformers, as, for example, Sir Patrick Hamilton, had been in touch with Wittenberg, but Knox, coming to Geneva, became a firm friend and admirer of Calvin, to remain in close touch with him throughout his life's work. Calvin realized fully how important for Protestantism was the struggle going on in Scotland and gave Knox all possible encouragement and support. Knox was on the continent for the four years 1554-1558. Before this he had already engaged with George Wishart in preaching the Reformation doctrine in Scotland, and after his period of suffering as a galley slave (1547-1549) had served as minister in England at Berwick, Newcastle and London.

His real work for Scotland began when the Protestants there laid the foundation of a definite organization in 1557. In that year " The Lords of the Congregation " covenanted with each other before God " that we shall with all diligence continually apply our whole power, substance, and our very lives to maintain, set forward and establish the most blessed Word of God and His congregation; and shall labour at our possibility to have faithful ministers purely and truly to minister Christ's evangel and sacraments to his people."[1] This was the first of the famous religious covenants, which later gave rise to the name of Covenanters. Two resolutions followed, namely, to use the prayer book of King Edward VI in parishes under their control, and to further the exposition of the Scriptures in private houses until the authorities permitted public preaching.

In 1559 these Lords of the Congregation took possession of Edinburgh, and began the establishment of Protestantism in Scotland. They first published the *Scotch Confession*, then passed laws abolishing the Pope's jurisdiction in the country, forbidding attendance at mass, and so forth. The reformed religion thus became recognized by legal authority, i.e., the authority of the Estates, though, of course, not of the sovereign. The *Scotch Confession* was Calvinistic in tone, and continued in use till superseded by the *Westminster Confession* about a century later.

The next phase in the struggle was the conflict with Mary Queen of Scots in which Knox played a leading part. It ended in a victory for Protestantism, a victory which had repercussions in most of the countries of Europe and not least in England. In some aspects it may be regarded as the most decisive victory for Protestantism in the western world, and it was a victory for the Genevan type of Protestantism. After it the Scots were free to organize their new church on Calvinistic lines.

The first *Book of Discipline* was issued in 1560. It

[1] T. M. Lindsay: *History of the Reformation*, Vol. II, p. 289.

L

provided for the government of the Church by Kirk-
sessions, synods, and general assemblies; and appointed
office bearers—ministers, teachers, elders, deacons,
superintendents and readers. This is the Calvinistic
organization, with certain additions, such as superintendents and readers, made necessary by the special
conditions existing in Scotland. The General Assembly
met for the first time in this same year 1560. Calvin's
Catechism for the young was translated and ordered to
be used. Also Knox's *Liturgy* superseded that of
Edward VI. From now on the work steadily proceeded
until all parishes were organized on the new model.

At a later stage the Second *Book of Discipline* was
issued (1578). This owed a great deal to Andrew
Melville, who also had first-hand acquaintance with
Geneva and the Reformed Church of the continent.
The Scotch organization was made still more Presbyterian by the establishment of Presbyteries to take the
place of the superintendents. " By 1580," says
Moffatt, " the General Assembly began to prefer
presbyteries to the limited autocracy of the superintendents, and by 1590 the final step of creating
presbyteries had been taken."[1]

As in Holland and Geneva, special attention was
given to education. Knox put forth ideas of a comprehensive system for the whole country, even including
a measure of compulsory education, but these remained
mainly as an ideal. Nevertheless, a great stimulus to
education resulted. The old universities, St. Andrew's,
Glasgow, and Aberdeen took on a new lease of life,
and a new one was founded at Edinburgh. These were
all staffed by men trained on the continent, most of
them at Geneva. Also attention on a wide scale was

[1] *Op. cit.* p. 52.

given to the education of the children in day schools in all parishes, with a carefully arranged system of teaching and inspection, in which, of course, the ministers took a leading part. The effect of these arrangements is seen in Scotland to-day in the respect paid to learning, in the thoroughly democratic conception of it, as well as in the connection which it still maintains with religion.

Another interesting feature of the Calvinism in Scotland lies in the fact that here for the first time was worked out the problem of fitting the organization to the national life as a whole. " Neither in France nor in Switzerland was it possible to show that Presbyterianism could develop a vital policy for the Church in national life. The opportunity of this fell to Scotland, and the passage of time proved that the Presbyterian constitution was as efficient and practical as the episcopal in England; in administrative self-government the Presbyterian polity indeed was second to none."[1] Moffatt points out how this necessity of fitting the organization to a national life led to modifications of the Genevan system—the Church of Scotland drawing freely upon other foreign Churches for both suggestions and precedents. Her debt to the French Protestant Church was particularly great. Indeed, Lindsay goes so far as to say that the Scottish organization owed more to France than to Geneva, the early organization, under Knox, being almost an exact reproduction of the French. He emphasizes the free popular element which was the strength of the early Scotch and French Churches, and which he points out modern Presbyterianism in both Great Britain and the United States of America has to some extent lost.[2]

[1] Moffatt: *Op. cit.* p. 56.
[2] Lindsay: *The Reformation* (Handbook for Bible Classes), p. 79.

There is no need here to follow further the development of the Presbyterian Church of Scotland, with its successful resistance to all attempts to force episcopacy upon the country, its abortive efforts after one united Presbyterian order in both England and Scotland, down to its fortunes in our own time. That it has contributed largely, out of all comparison to its size, to the enrichment of Christian life and thought is well known. Particularly in the realms of scholarship and preaching has it shown remarkable virility and brilliance. Needless to say, there has been, within the years, much modification of the original dogmatic scheme, but the Church remains Calvinistic in its organization and in its underlying church-idea. Its contribution to the church-idea is well summed up by Moffatt—" What these three centuries in Scotland have done for Presbyterianism, therefore, has mainly been to elucidate in terms of modern thought and practice the dominant conception of the Church. The exigencies of the situation have led to this being defined in relation to the State, with a success to which there is no parallel in any other country. But the central idea underneath the long, painful struggle . . . was the Presbyterian belief in the Church as at once a divine institution, with freedom to govern itself, and also as the Church of the nation, with relations and responsibilities to the State."[1]

One other effect of Scotch Calvinism has been the widespread influence of devout Scots who have settled in different parts of the world. The story of religion in America, and notably in our British colonies, as well as in some other countries, brings a well-deserved tribute to men from beyond the border who have carried their Presbyterian organization and spirit to

[1] *Op. cit.* p. 80.

the lands of their adoption. The pioneering Scot (and where has he not pioneered?) has often been an emissary of John Calvin, and the Reformer was right, more than he knew, in regarding Scotland as one of the most important victories won for the Reformation.

An illustration of this missionary activity near at home is furnished by the Presbyterianism in Ireland. It dates from the plantation of Ulster by James I, and was due to the large Scottish element of the new population.   There the Presbyterians at first drew close to the Episcopalians who had come from England, and in 1615 Archbishop Usher admitted the validity of Presbyterian ordination and denied the distinction between bishop and presbyter. After the rebellion of 1641, however, the Protestant Church in Ireland was almost ruined until a revival took place largely stimulated by the Presbyterian ministers of Scottish regiments stationed in the country. Kirk-sessions were formed in four regiments and the first regular presbytery held in 1642 at Carrickfergus. Ministers were brought over from Scotland and the Church of Ulster firmly established (1643). After the Restoration an attempt was made to suppress the Church, and the ministers were ejected. Later, however, 1665, the ministers were again allowed to organize Presbyterian worship and the Church was firmly established, to continue both vigorous and vocal to the present day.

II. CALVINISM IN ENGLAND

In the English story the chief features are the decisive rejection of Presbyterianism as a system for the religious life of the nation as a whole with the consequent decline of such Presbyterian Churches as succeeded in establishing themselves, and then also the permeating influence of Calvinism affecting, for a time, almost every section of the country's Protestant life. Broadly speaking we may say that England refused to adopt Calvinism as an ecclesiastical system while it drank deep of the Calvinistic theology and ethic. Presbyterianism was rejected, but Puritanism flourished.

On the purely religious side Calvin's influence steadily spread until for a time it became dominant. The Reformer himself did not cease—to quote his own phrase —to have an eye to the condition of the kingdom. On the accession of Edward VI he wrote to Protector Somerset making suggestions, all of which were adopted. Also he had correspondence with the King and with Cranmer. To Edward VI he dedicated his commentary on *Isaiah*. However, it was through his pupils he exercised his greatest influence, men like Martin Bucer, Paul Fagius, Peter Martyr, and Bernard Ochino, all Calvinists teaching at the universities during Edward's reign. Thus it came about that the *Thirty-nine Articles* of Elizabeth's time, still operative in the Church of England, have a Calvinistic tone, especially in the doctrines of the eucharist and predestination. The persecution under Queen Mary again sent many good men to the continent, and most of these came under the influence of Calvin and returned later to occupy important positions in the Church of Elizabeth. From this group also came the Genevan Bible, a family Bible with Calvinistic notes both doctrinal and practical, of which no less than 140 editions were published before 1644. Under these influences the actual doctrines of Calvin were steadily presented throughout England and Scotland; and in a short time came to be regarded as standard.[1] They ruled in the Anglican Church till the time of Archbishop Laud, and for a much longer period in the Dissenting bodies. The *Institutes* was several times translated and became the foundation of English theological learning, while, as a commentator, Calvin long maintained his position in all branches of the English Protestant Church.

The determined attempt to make the Presbyterian organization national was made in the reign of Elizabeth. It was connected with the growth of the Puritan party which now began its remarkable career in the western world. In its first phase Puritanism concerned itself chiefly with the ceremonies of the Church, aiming at simplicity in worship by getting rid of all " rags of popery." Many in the party believed that this could be attained without sacrificing episcopacy, but over against these was a vocal section who preferred the Genevan order. Of these the leader was Thomas Cartwright,[2] who went so far as to maintain that Scripture both teaches and enjoins a definite church-polity, and that the Presbyterian. He and his friends established a presbytery or kirk-sessions at Wandsworth in 1572. Their outlook carried with it, of course, the idea that Christ alone is the head of his Church, and that the civil magistrate and even the monarch is not exempt from spiritual discipline. At this vital point it was clean contrary to the settled policy of Elizabeth and the Stuarts. After many attempts the effort finally failed, and under the Stuarts Presbyterianism receded, carrying with it a prejudice against

[1] W. T. Whitley: *Calvinism and Evangelism in England*, p. 5.
[2] *v.* A. F. Scott Pearson: *Thomas Cartwright and Elizabethan Puritanism.*

it in the mind of the average Englishman. The two phrases, that of King James from the side of monarchist absolutism, " No bishop, no king," and that of Milton, breathing the spirit of rising democracy, " New presbyter is but old priest writ large," are sufficient indication of the points of view of the different parties who opposed it. The issue thus presented, namely, whether the religious life of the country should be ordered on episcopal or presbyterian lines was decided once for all in favour of the former. Afterwards Presbyterianism in England declined and its churches languished, though new churches were established at a later date.

One lasting benefit from this phase of the struggle, however, was the *Westminster Confession* produced by the Westminster Assembly in 1643-4. The Assembly was called by Cromwell to advise as to a new form of Church government, and though it failed to get its elaborate scheme for a Presbyterian order for the Church in England adopted, it issued the *Confession*, which is one of the outstanding statements of Calvinism and still one of the standards of the Presbyterian Church. The Assembly also produced the *Larger* and *Shorter Catechisms* and the *Directory of Public Worship*. This latter has had great influence on the forms of worship in many parts of the Protestant Anglo-Saxon world.

However, while the ecclesiastical system was rejected, the influence of the theology and the ethical emphasis was far-reaching. To-day, now that old controversies are forgotten and the issues blurred, the word Puritanism means, for many, simply a certain rigorous kind of life, in the main an ethical outlook. The word carries with it ideas of stern self-discipline, simplicity of manners with a scrupulous care of money, concentration on duty, and what is in many quarters regarded as an unduly strict and narrow code of morals. This attitude to life undoubtedly derives from Calvinism, though of course it could be held along with variations from the strict Calvinistic theology. It was already taking possession of Puritanism in the latter part of Elizabeth's reign. After the excitement of the Spanish war had passed, and in the prosperity which flooded the country in the spacious years of expansion, there was a decline of morals which stirred the best minds to strong reaction. Hence the old Puritanism with its interest in Church garments and forms of worship was transformed. To a new generation of thoughtful men the conflict against immorality and vice loomed larger even than the fight against Rome. " They desired that under the teaching of the Bible, interpreted as it was then through the medium of the Calvinistic theology, every Englishman should devote himself to the fulfilment of those duties in which they saw the worthy preparation for the life to come. . . . It was by its demand for a purer morality that Puritanism retained its hold upon the laity."[1]

Thus the new Puritanism was to a large extent developed over against what Henson calls " the aggressiveness of foreign vice." This may account for the insularity that has always attached to it. It was essentially an English product though capable of being to some extent transplanted. In the reign of James such an outlook inevitably became the expression of the best conscience of the nation. By the scandal of his court, the publication of *The Book of Sports*, and other such acts James fell foul of the public

[1] S. R. Gardiner: *History of England*, Vol. III, p. 239. Quoted H. Hensley Henson: *Puritanism in England*, p. 45.

conscience, and in doing so placed the Episcopal
Church on the wrong side. So that Puritanism
with its strong ethical emphasis became synonymous
with patriotism, and to some extent anti-Anglican.
Baxter is the outstanding example of this second
generation of Puritans. He records how he saw
a stage play instead of a sermon on the Lord's Day,
and heard little preaching, and such as there was mainly
against the Puritans. His statement about his father
gives the atmosphere of the time and admirably illustrates the real strength of the party—" When I heard
them call my father Puritan it did much to alienate me
from them . . . when I heard my own father so re-
proached and perceived the drunkards were the for-
wardest in the reproach, I perceived that it was mere
malice. For my father never scrupled common prayer
or ceremonies, nor spake against bishops, nor ever so
much as prayed but by a book or form, being not ever
acquainted then with any that did otherwise; but only
for reading Scripture when the rest were dancing on
the Lord's Day and for praying . . . in his house, and
for reproving drunkards and swearers, and for talking
sometimes a few words of Scripture and the life to
come, he was reviled commonly by the name Puritan,
Precisian, and hypocrite."[1] It is interesting to note
that even a man of the world like Pepys the diarist
was capable at times of feeling something of the same
sentiment. Speaking of the play *Bartholomew Fair*, he
writes, " The more I see it the more I love the wit of it;
only the business of abusing the Puritans begins to
grow stale, and of no use, they being the people that,
at the last will be found the wisest."[2]

Under the Stuarts many of the Puritans were driven

[1] *Life*, quoted Henson, *op. cit.* p. 55 f.   [2] *Diary* September 4th, 1668.

into Nonconformity, the Calvinism of which was further strengthened by their presence (nearly all the 2,000 clergy who were ejected in 1662 were Calvinists).[1] The Baptists and the Congregationalists, who with the Presbyterians formed the backbone of this Nonconformity, owed not a little to Calvin's formulation of the idea of the spiritual autonomy of the Church under Christ as the sole head, and both denominations, more or less, remained under the dominance of the theology of the *Institutes* until the time when the Wesleyan revival with its Arminian emphasis began to make itself felt.[1] The exceptions were the General Baptists who were Arminian from the first, and the Quakers, who were probably as little influenced by Geneva as any Christian body in England. Towards the end of the seventeenth century the reign of the dogmatic system began to be relaxed, the Church of England had already moved away in part from the Calvinistic presentation, and most religious bodies tended towards Latitudinarianism. In the eighteenth century the religious life of the nation came under the dominance of new forces, and to a large extent the Puritan wave had spent itself, though its influence was still to be felt in certain aspects of both the religious and political life. Calvinism, however, remained as a living creed in its conflict with Arminianism well on into the nineteenth century.[2]

Concerning Calvinism as an influence on the growth of English democracy it is not possible here to write at any length, but it is a point not to be overlooked. As in France, there was opposition to the absolutism of the

---

[1] W. T. Whitley: *Op. cit.* p. 11. Cf. also M. Piette: *John Wesley in the Evolution of Protestantism*, Book II, pt. 2.
[2] A. W. Harrison : *Op. cit.* cap. VIII.

sovereign, which, while it may not have been caused entirely by the new view in religion, was nevertheless greatly reinforced by it. The precise part played by Calvinism in the struggle would be a matter of debate, but if the Reformation generally gave men first the idea of ecclesiastical liberty and then that of political freedom, it was the Calvinistic type that wrought in this direction in the practical politics of the world. Nor was England an exception. M. Piette goes so far as to regard the revolution of 1688 as the complete triumph of Calvinism after a century and a half of struggle.[1] Perhaps this is too sweeping a judgment, but certain it is, that the whole political development in the troubled years of the Stuarts owed not a little to the Genevan spirit of organization and even more to the stern sense of duty with regard to the State which the theology everywhere inculcated. Calvinism was a fighting creed and it was not found wanting when vital issues had to be determined. The fact that political and religious questions were so closely allied and even confused in the days when the foundations of English democracy were laid contributed much to the distinctive English outlook. One has only to contrast the impact of religion on social life in England and America with the comparative lack of it in Roman Catholic countries such as Italy and Spain, or for that matter Germany itself with its Lutheran quietism, to realize that in this direction Calvinism has been no negligible factor. Again and again in England it has been found impossible to separate politics from religion. And this aggressiveness of religion in the sphere of government and social life, which continued well on into the nineteenth century, particularly amongst the Nonconform-

[1] *Op. cit.* p. 94.

ists, undoubtedly goes back to the earlier grounding of the common people in Calvinistic principles.

Here we note also that our national literature bears abundant witness to the permeating influence of Calvinism, even though little of it actually came from strictly Calvinistic circles. John Henry Newman, even with Shakespeare in mind, has pointed out that English literature is essentially Protestant,[1] and Edward Dowden[2] specifies more particularly when he writes— " Continental, if not English critics, have recognized the fact that a Puritan strain has entered into much that is most characteristic in our literature. It is present in the *Faerie Queen* as well as in *Samson Agonistes*; in the *Vision of Sin,* the *Palace of Art,* the *Idylls of the King*; in the poetry of the author of *Dipsychus* and the poetry of the author of *Christmas Eve and Easter Day*; in the prose of *Sartor Resartus.* And though Matthew Arnold said hard things, and some of them not without good reason, of English Puritanism, the son of Thomas Arnold could not escape from an hereditary influence; the Hellenic tendency in his poetry is constantly checked and controlled by the Hebraic tendency as it had been accepted and modified by the English mind."

In addition to this Puritan strain, which obviously has counted for a great deal, Milton and Bunyan particularly may be mentioned as being direct channels of Calvinism itself to the English mind. Milton's very purpose of attempting " to justify the ways of God to man " by the unfolding of the plan of salvation is pure Calvinism, and indeed his great work might almost be regarded as the Calvinistic scheme done into blank verse, this in spite of his opposition to the Presbyterians

[1] *Idea of a University,* p. 314.   [2]*Puritan and Anglican,* p. 14.

and also of the fact that at points he modified the
theology. One could easily imagine that the *Institutes*
itself suggested the scheme of the poem if not the title—
Paradise Lost.

Bunyan is significant if only for the phenomenal
circulation of his masterpiece. His general outlook is
definitely that of English Calvinism. He probably did
more than any other to make that outlook, both theological and ethical, run through the countryside, nor
could his work be entirely undone at a later time by the
assiduous itineraries of Wesley.

The very name of Bunyan is a reminder of the
striking fact that Calvinism succeeded in giving a fairly
uniform theological background to the common mind.
The majority came to accept almost unconsciously the
theological ideas even including predestination, till in
the seventeenth century practically the whole Protestant thinking of the country was conditioned by the Calvinistic outlook. In this sense, Calvinism created in
England, at least for a time, a unity of outlook not unlike that which the Roman Catholic Church gave to the
Middle Ages. And when to this was added the Puritan
ethical emphasis, the conditions were present for the
birth of that tone and temper, which makes it possible
for statesmen even yet to make a high moral appeal with
the certainty of a widespread response, and which, be
it said, often wins for England abroad the name of
hypocrite. Considering all these factors we may truly
say that, even in Calvin's own lifetime, the movement
began which was destined to make his life's work one
of the shaping influences of the Anglo-Saxon world.
His theology counted for much, his ethics for more, and
perhaps the spirit and temper of his system for most
of all.

III. Calvinism in the New World

In its pure form Calvinism was taken across the Atlantic by the Dutch and by the Scotch, both Presbyterian and Reformed Churches being established. But, in addition to this, the modified Calvinism of the English sects went with the early settlers, and had profound effect in moulding both the constitution and life-forms of the new country. From the beginning religion played a great part in the development, and it meant a great deal that this religion was Protestantism, and, moreover, Protestantism of the Calvinistic kind. In the new country, naturally, there was a freer development, unhampered by earlier national traditions, and hence we expect considerable modifications in the application of Calvinistic ideas. But the general background of thought remained Calvinistic. Lewis S. Mudge estimates that, at the time of the War of Independence, about two million of the three million inhabitants of the thirteen states were of Calvinistic stock.[1] This does not mean that they derived from Presbyterians as such, but rather were descendants of early settlers of Calvinistic type. Allowing full weight to this permeating influence of Calvin's theology and ethical emphasis, we may say that nowhere did the system produce its distinctive type more clearly than in the United States. It was indeed a creed for colonists. Its very hardness seemed to match the conditions of life, its doctrine of predestination and election, with its disparagement of weakly sentimentality, bred a spirit of self-sufficiency and independence, a feeling of personal power, while its ethics combined admirably with the pioneer spirit in an expanding world of trade

[1] *Encyclopaedia Britannica*, Edition XIV, Vol. XVIII, p. 447.

and commerce. If it is at all true, as some maintain, that Calvinism lies at the back of the bourgeoisie, then the development in this direction is best illustrated in the history of the United States of America.

Also it must be noticed that the solutions indicated in Calvinism for some of the practical problems of life, as, for example, that of the relation of Church and State, and also that of the ordering of the common life with a view to stability, offered real guidance to men making a fresh start. The settlers were bound to model their new State to some extent on the pattern of the old, but as many of them had left the old in order to win a new freedom, they started out predisposed to lay better foundations and to build in a new way. Certainly not all the State-builders of the new world took Calvin consciously as guide, but many of them, and those the section which became finally most influential, obviously owed him a great debt. In the end, some of his characteristic ideas came to permanent power in the constitution of the United States. Indeed, the writer quoted above goes so far as to say—" The form of government of our nation is practically the form of government of the Presbyterian Church with such modifications as the civil sphere requires."[1]

From this point of view of national influence the important section was that of the English Puritans, especially the Congregationalists who settled in New England. Although not Presbyterians, and, indeed at some points strongly opposed to that body, they were nevertheless distinctly Calvinistic in their theology and general outlook, and it is easy to mark the Calvinistic features of their earliest arrangements. Thus they did

[1] Mudge: *Op. cit.* p. 447.

not begin with the idea of religious toleration. As Troeltsch says, Calvinistic Congregationalists alone were recognized.[1] They emphasized genuine conversion as the mark of the Christian, and they attached the most important civil rights to Church membership. For example, in Massachusetts Bay and afterwards in New Haven Colony, the right to vote and hold office was restricted to members of the Church. Here we have still the conception of the theocratic community. Even in a Colony such as Connecticut, where the suffrage was not so limited, the interests of religion were carefully guarded in the constitution. In fact, nowhere was religion ignored. Generally, the State had the duty of repressing heresy and schism, and of attending to any abuse in the management of the Church. In New Haven Colony the laws of Moses were provisionally adopted as a civil code. As to the government of the Church itself, it was claimed that the Church had the right of self-government, but the Churches were linked together by councils. In no sense were they isolated units. The councils, it is true, were not authoritative as were the Presbyterians' synods, but exerted only an advisory function. The arrangement was indeed a sort of compromise between Congregationalism and Presbyterianism, but it shows the characteristic Presbyterian aim of endeavouring to combine an authoritative central body with a measure of local freedom.

Then in the matter of the ordering of the life of the individuals in the community, the Puritan ethic was ready to hand to meet what obviously was an urgent need. The problem was to create an ordered communal life, and this, often, out of very stubborn

[1] *Op. cit.* Vol. II, p. 666.

M

individualistic personalities. This task was generally
attempted by the promulgation of a code of morals
enforced by the State and by religious education.
Thus, at a later time, in Georgia for example, even
before that region came under the dominance of the
Baptists, acts were passed for preventing and punishing
vice, profaneness, and immorality, and for keeping the
Lord's Day holy. Anyone failing to keep the Day and
frequent some place of worship was to be fined. No
one to work on Sunday, and nothing to be sold but
milk and fish. No hunting, plays or games. Public-
houses to be closed and church wardens to inspect them
twice each Sunday. No travel except to church or for
visiting the sick. The magistrates to meet on each
first Monday of every third month to hear complaints
concerning violation of these laws of religion.[1] It is a
far cry from Geneva in the sixteenth century to
Georgia in the eighteenth, but the spirit is the same.
It means that Calvinism offered a ready way of dealing
with a practical situation. And a similar spirit operated
throughout the colonies, though, naturally, with local
variations of expression. Everywhere the close cooperation of Church and State in the care of religion,
respect for the Bible, Sabbatarianism, the crystalliza-
tion of religion into a legalistic code, which was as
much in the interests of the State as of the Church. It
may well be that one of the reasons why this spirit
persisted in the United States almost to our own time,
was that it had served the colonists so well in the days
of their first need. It was these men of Calvinistic
stock who were the backbone of the revolution which
led to independence.[2] So that Calvinism is in the life

[1] R. C. Strickland: *Religion and State in Georgia in the eighteenth
century*, p. 129.   [2] Cf. Moffatt: *Op. cit.* p. 88.

blood of the nation and, as we have seen, something of it went even into the final constitution.

Here from our point of view is one of the main points of interest in the story of Calvinism in America. We have seen it modifying the constitutions and life-forms of old established countries in Switzerland, Holland and Great Britain, but here we have it operating as a chief factor in creating a new State. The influence of the United States in the world to-day makes its origins a matter of great interest. These origins reveal one of the most spectacular triumphs of Calvinism.

At a later period the earlier Calvinism was again quickened by the Great Awakening. This movement, it is true, brought new forces into the old outlook, akin to the Pietism of Germany and the Methodism of England, and it was opposed particularly by the Universities of Harvard and Yale. But out of it eventually came the theology of Jonathan Edwards (1703-1758). In spite of his modifications of the original Calvinistic position, Edwards remained essentially a Calvinist, the absolute divine sovereignty in conversion and man's total inability being his cardinal doctrines. He founded a school of theology which had great influence for many years, and his work undoubtedly gave Calvinism a new lease of life in the States. How far Whitefield's tours in 1739-40 helped in the same direction is not so easy to say. By his ministrations many thousands were converted and the spiritual condition of many communities greatly improved. But though Whitefield was Calvinist in his theology, as against Wesley's Arminianism, it is probable that the real effect of his preaching was in the direction of the wider view. His evangelistic zeal and his enthusiastic appeal to all without distinction probably outweighed his formal theology. However, many Churches already Calvinistic before the revival still remained so afterwards, yet were all the better and more vigorous for the quickening which the revival had brought. In the end, of course, America felt the influence of the spreading Arminianism and Romanticism, though this came later there than in England, and less radically than in the more confined space of the homeland.

The full Calvinistic organization as such is represented in the United States by the Presbyterian Church and also by branches of the Reformed Church.

The earliest Presbyterians were Huguenots who went to Port Royal in 1562, and to Florida in 1564. The first church of British origin was established in 1617, and during the latter half of the seventeenth century churches of a Presbyterian type were founded in many of the States, notably in the middle colonies. During the first half of the eighteenth century many Presbyterians arrived from Ulster, and one of these, Francis Makemie, is regarded as the pioneer of the present-day Presbyterian Church in the country. He itinerated widely from New York to the Carolinas, establishing Presbyterian Churches, and in 1705 organized the first real presbytery known as the Presbytery of Philadelphia. He was chosen as first moderator. The first meeting of the synod was held in 1717, and the synod in 1729 adopted the *Westminster Confession* and the *Larger* and *Shorter Catechisms*, thus bringing the Church into line with historic Presbyterianism. Since that day the cause has grown enormously, having great influence both in the national life of the United States and in the Presbyterian Church throughout the world.

The Reformed Dutch Church in America traces its origin to Dutch settlers who founded a trading colony on the site where New York now stands. There they formed the first Dutch Reformed Church in 1628. The Church has steadily increased with the years. Its standards are the *Belgic Confession*, the *Heidelberg Catechism* and the decrees of the Synod of Dort.

Akin to it is the Reformed Church of the United States, a German Calvinistic community tracing its origin to Switzerland and Germany, and especially to the great influx of Germans to Pennsylvania in the seventeenth century.

It is not possible to follow further the fortunes of the Presbyterian Church in the British Colonies and also in its various mission fields. Suffice it to say that it is found to-day in every part of the Christian world, and though it has modified the theology and adapted the organization to varying conditions, the original spirit of Calvinism is still present. The Reformer's leading ideas and his earnest purposes are still enshrined in active communities which are contributing to the higher life of mankind. The *Institutes* as a comprehensive statement of Protestant doctrine has been compared not unjustly with the *Summa* of Thomas Aquinas; but, as against the Church of Rome, Calvinism did not succeed in building up a world-organization, nor did the organization itself spread uniformly with the outlook. All the same, it will not be forgotten that it did much to teach ordinary men to organize, to set them to the task, and to supply them with guiding lines for it. For this, if for nothing more, Protestantism and the democracies of the world owe the Genevan Reformer an incalculable debt.

PART III

SOME ASPECTS OF CALVINISM

CHAPTER X

THE CALVINISTIC VIEW OF SCRIPTURE

ONE of the obvious differences between the religious world before and after the Reformation was the new attitude to the Bible. Of that fact the translations of it into the various languages are sufficient proof. But if it is true that the Reformation rediscovered the Bible it is equally true that it was Calvinism which secured and consolidated the gains of that discovery. A generation after Luther the Bible occupies an entirely new place in the thoughts and affections of men largely owing to the place given to it in the Calvinistic theology and to the spread of that theology in the Western world.

It is often said that the Reformation put the Bible in the seat of authority in place of Pope and Church, and though such a statement needs qualification so far as the leaders themselves are concerned,[1] yet it stands as a fair statement of fact for the majority of those who accepted the new outlook. This was inevitable if only because of the place given to the Book in the controversy with Roman Catholicism. The Reformers one and all stood on it as basis in the attack on Rome, believing to find in it the new ideas which were the solvent of Rome's claims, and that primitive simplicity to which it was held the Church needed to return. Hence so long as these ideas were living issues and the controversy continued, for this reason if for no other, the Bible was sure to retain its place, and the very condi-

---

[1] v. G. Jackson: *In a Preacher's Study*, cap. I.

tions of the controversy made it necessary to ascribe
to it a complete authority. Thus it remained for a
long period a chief source of light, the one justification
of the new opinions, and the irrefutable authority
replacing both the Church and Aristotle.

However, its influence went far beyond the arena of
this particular controversy. The book now became
part of the common heritage of men. In the first flush
of enthusiasm it was appealed to on political issues
quite as readily as on theological. Milton's attitude is
typical of the educated. When he defends the action
taken against Charles I he quotes Biblical precedents
as justification, citing *Deuteronomy*, *Ecclesiastes* and
Joshua to prove that the King also is bound by law,
and the incident of Rehoboam for the right of the
people to reject their king.[1] Thus expositions of the
Bible at considerable length are mixed with political
arguments, and the writer is obviously conscious that
such illustrations are weighty to the minds of at least
that section for whom he writes. Nor does he for one
moment doubt either the relevance or the authority of
the Scripture in such matters. That is to say the
Bible has now become a guide in the fullest sense of
the term for thinking men. Indeed, in the two
centuries following the Reformation every branch
of learning, not excluding science, felt the influence
of the Bible and had to take account of its
existence. The way in which its thoughts, not to
mention its language, have intertwined themselves in
English classic literature is well known. We must not
overlook the fact that it was one of the gifts of the
Renaissance, and was received as such by the intellectual classes. It opened to them vistas of a new world

Defense of the People of England.

of thought not incomparable with the marvellous material world which the young science was now beginning to unfold. Sir Isaac Newton, turning aside from his mathematics to deal with the question of biblical chronology and to write a book on the prophecies of *Daniel* and the *Revelation*,[1] may have been in this respect somewhat exceptional, but certain it is that to the men of his time the serious study of the Bible and the scanning of the heavenly bodies were disciplines not so far apart as they are to-day. The book in its first discovery changed men's perspective. It was a real factor in the newly-awakening intellectual life, and withal it brought an extraordinary sense of emancipation.

However, even more important from our point of view at the moment is the fact that the Bible became the property of the common man. It was translated and placed in the churches to be read. And it was read. Indeed, it stimulated the very desire to read. The assumptions were that the common man had the right to read it, and also that he had the intellect both to understand what he read and to interpret it. Scripture is clear, Calvin maintained, it is God's will to enlighten the humble, and if we come in humility nothing useful for our salvation will be obscure.[2] We have seen that the Reformer held that the common man could not be served without the Scripture. It was put on the level of daily bread and the knowledge of it made a necessity. Incidentally, the average man was made a combatant in controversy, encouraged to enquire and to investigate the evidence, and then to utter his mind. Thus it was the new attitude in religion which for the first time

[1] O. Lodge: *Pioneers of Science*, p. 201. It is interesting to note that Napier, the inventor of logarithms, also wrote a book on the *Revelation* which went into Dutch, French and German editions.

[2] *v.* Doumergue: *Op. cit.* Vol. IV, p. 81.

made him vocal. And here we have the beginning
both of general education and of that awakening of the
mind of the average man which is the foundation of
democracy. " For now the time seems come," says
Milton in the *Areopagitica*, " wherein Moses the great
prophet may sit in heaven rejoicing to see that memor-
able and glorious wish of his fulfilled when not only the
seventy elders but all the Lord's people are become
prophets." Some would say that it only filled the
world with noisy clamour and gave voice to a great
multitude of ignoramuses, and this is true enough; but
the temporary chaos in the realm of opinion, which was
the first manifestation of this new freedom, must not
be allowed to blind our eyes to the ultimate value of the
freedom itself. Milton was right surely in discerning
that something of great significance had happened in
the world. Opinion in good men, he maintains, is but
knowledge in the making. It is scarcely too much to
say that the beginning of the emancipation of the mind
in modern times lies in this encouragement of every
man to read and use the Bible for himself,—" to take
the care of his religion into his own hands," in Milton's phrase. All this we owe to the Reformation but
particularly to the work of Calvin. That Calvin saw
the full significance of it no one, of course, would claim,
still less that he himself intended all these consequences.
Indeed, could he have foreseen one wonders whether
he would not have been profoundly disturbed, so great
is the difference of his own actual view-point from that
which finally developed. But it is the fact that Calvin's
view of Scripture contained in it this great possibility
of development, and it is this which makes it so interesting and important for a study of the shaping forces
of the modern world.

What then is Calvin's view?

He begins his *Institutes* as we have seen with a statement of what is usually called natural religion. God has revealed Himself in His works. But unfortunately, owing to sin, man is not capable of reading this revelation or profiting by it. Hence some better guide had to be given to enable man to reach that knowledge of God which is essential to salvation. Therefore God added the light of His Word. Thus the Scripture is regarded theoretically as a supplement to the common natural proofs, but since we cannot in the least profit by these proofs it becomes actually a necessity, " a surer and more direct means of discovering God." In fact, for practical purposes it is the only means. " If true religion is to beam upon us, our principle must be that it is necessary to begin with the heavenly teaching, and that it is impossible for anyone to obtain even the minutest portion of right and sound doctrine without being a disciple of Scripture " (I.vi.2).

This judgment is based on the doctrine of Scripture as the infallible Word of God. It is the very Word which God has spoken for the enlightenment of the elect. Thus Calvin can use such phrases as " God's own voice " (I.vii.1), " dictated by the Holy Spirit " (IV.viii.5) and of the writers " authentic amanuenses of the Holy Spirit " (IV.viii.9). Doumergue insists that Calvin used such phrases without intending an inspiration " mécanique, litteral, verbale,"[1] and it would certainly give a false impression to say that he held by verbal infallibility.[2] At the same time he firmly insists on the fact that the Bible as a whole is both infallible

---

[1] *Op. cit.* Vol. IV, p. 76.
[2] " Trifling discrepancies in the sacred narrative he treated with light-hearted unconcern." Jackson: *Op. cit.* p. 21.

and authoritative. The truth is given in Scripture once
for all, and the Bible is " such a depository of doctrine
as would secure the truth from perishing from neglect,
vanishing amid error, or being corrupted by the pre-
sumptuous audacity of men " (I.vi.3). Thus truth is
regarded as fixed and static, capable of being put in
the pages of a book and handed down from generation
to generation. Nay, the book-form is its safeguard.
Calvin admits that not every word of Scripture leads
to faith (III.ii.7), but the modern distinction between
the Bible and the Word of God in the Bible is one that
he does not make.

We have to admit that the general drift of his
teaching, at least for the mass of men, was in the
direction of verbal infallibility even though he himself
put the emphasis on the larger whole. Even Milton in
quoting *Deuteronomy* in the passage referred to above
writes—" First let us hear God Himself speak." This
is quite in the manner of Calvin. But clearly such a
mode of speech and the outlook it implies leads easily
to the doctrine of verbal infallibility, and it had the
effect of making the Bible a book of proof-texts with
the habit of regarding almost any text as decisive
argument.

Then secondly, Scripture is not only necessary but
sufficient. Everything pertaining to Christianity is
prescribed and contained in it (IV.xix.9). " The Word
of the Lord is the only way which can conduct us to
the investigation of whatever it is lawful for us to
know with regard to Him . . . the only light which
enables us to discern what we ought to see with regard
to Him . . . it will curb and restrain all presumption "
(III.xxi.2). Without it we inevitably turn vain in our
imaginations. More, God has confined us to His Word.

Everything pertaining to a perfect rule of life He has so comprehended in His law that He has left nothing for men to add to the summary there given (IV.x.7). Nothing therefore is safer than to banish all the boldness of human sense and adhere solely to what the Scripture delivers (IV.xviii.12).

There are passages in the *Institutes* which taken out of their context might almost seem to suggest that the Reformer was willing to confine men to Scripture entirely, as though nothing profitable could be found in any other place. But a consideration of his own educational system at Geneva alone is enough to refute such an idea. By the sufficiency of Scripture he means sufficiency for salvation, and he elaborates the idea naturally on the background of the religious controversies of the time. His thought is that the Church can add nothing that is not there already, the experience of the ages can do no more than further elucidate the Bible. However, while he finds room for the wider outlook and thus saves himself from obscurantism, he still holds that salvation is pre-eminently man's main concern, and since all that is required for it is in the Scripture and in the Scripture only, this becomes of supreme importance to him and its study a matter of earnest necessity. Such an emphasis had the effect undoubtedly in the earlier days of limited education of stimulating many to become " men of one book," as the phrase went, inhibiting to that extent a more liberal education. But in this Calvinism was responsible only for the earnestness and not for the actual limitation itself. Speaking in general terms all would agree that Presbyterians as a body have not been wanting in the furtherance of liberal studies, even though their Church like most others has known its

proscriptions for heresy. Those who at a later time
insisted on finding their science in the Bible and in no
other place were rather at another point. They were
actually fighting for the doctrine of verbal infallibility.

The third point in Calvin's treatment of Scripture is
that it is a unity, made so by the fact that all and every
part of it is concerned with the one purpose, namely,
the setting forth of the mediator Christ. This follows
from the place given to Christ in the divine economy.
If he comes to fuller expression in the New Testament,
nevertheless, it is he who is presented also in the Old.
There is no saving knowledge of God without Christ,
and consequently he was held forth to all the elect as
the one object of their faith and confidence from the
very beginning of history (II.vi.4). So in familiarizing
the Jews with the prophecies and psalms, " God intended to teach them that in seeking for deliverance
they should turn their eyes directly towards Christ "
(*idem*). The only way by which in ancient times holy
men knew God was by beholding Him in the Son as in
a mirror, nor did God ever manifest Himself by any
other means than by His Son.

From this very fountain it was that Adam, Noah,
Abraham, Isaac, Jacob all drew such heavenly doctrine
as they possessed (IV.viii.5). The law itself is thus a
manifestation of Christ, while the prophets are only
interpreters of the Law, and can add nothing to it save
predictions of future events. Then when at last the
Wisdom of God was manifested in the flesh he fully
unfolded to us all that the human mind can comprehend or ought to think of the heavenly Father
(IV.viii.7). This revelation in His son was complete
and final, so that even the apostles, like the prophets
of old, could do no more than expound the ancient

Scriptures and show that the things there delivered are fulfilled in Christ. They were to teach only what he commanded and merely to bring to remembrance what he had said to them. " This restriction," says Calvin, " should be carefully attended to " (Iv.viii.8).

Calvin thus makes a certain distinction between the Old Testament and the New,[1] giving the New the higher place because of the account of the earthly life of our Lord, but there is in his theory no true historic sense and no allowance for any human element. All Scripture teaches the same thing even though all is not on the same level. In this sense at least the Old Testament is of equal authority with the New and the Decalogue as binding as the Sermon on the Mount. Calvin himself sees the Church everywhere in Scripture and uses texts from the *Psalms* or *Isaiah* or *Malachi* on a level with those of the New Testament as being equally applicable to the life of the Church of his own day and for all time. It is this indiscriminate use of Scripture which causes his writings to wear such an antiquated aspect to the modern reader, who now finds so many of the quotations simply irrelevant to the matter in hand.

It will be seen that Calvin saves the Old Testament for Christianity by very much the same considerations as weighed with the Church of the second century in its conflict with Judaism and Gnosticism. We value the book to-day because we have a more adequate conception of a progressive revelation. It reveals the gradual growth of those religious ideas which were destined to flower in Christianity. To Calvin, with no such clue in mind, the Old Testament could only be of value as it was regarded as bearing direct testimony to

[1] See *Inst*. Book II.x.xi.

N

Christ. He thus makes Christ central in the whole of
Scripture in a way that is scarcely possible to a modern
thinker. This made it appear a unity incapable of
contradicting itself, and this certainly was the strength
of the theory.

Its weakness is obvious. It places the Old Testament
on a level with the New with very serious consequences
especially on the ethical side. This, as is well known, is
one of the obvious distinguishing marks of Calvinism
in general. Also the theory at this point again makes
in the direction of a mechanical conception of inspiration. Another weakness was that it made the Bible
a compendium of theology and gave it a purely theological interpretation, thus obscuring for a long time
its more human qualities.

However, the theory led to one immediate gain. It
made exegesis necessary and produced a new type.
Calvin himself wrote commentaries on almost all the
books of the Bible and left a tradition in this respect
which has not yet ceased to operate. His view of
Scripture put an end to the fantastic and allegorical
types of exegesis which had prevailed in the Middle
Ages, and made in the direction of an honest attempt
to get at the real meaning, " the sense most true and
natural."[1] His principles of exegesis are recognized as
in the main sound. The chief excellence of the inter-
preter consists in " perspicuous brevity." " And indeed
since it is almost his whole business to lay open the
mind of the writer whom he intends to interpret, if he
withdraws his hearers from that, he so far turns aside
from his main end or at least wanders beyond his
limits."[2] When we recall that Calvin's example was

[1] Cf. Commentary on *1 Cor.* v. 9.
[2] Preface to *Romans. v.* Tholuck: *Merits of Calvin*, p. 14.

followed not only by scholars, but by a whole multitude of preachers in every country where Calvinism spread, we see that in this regard he did a genuine service both to theology and religion. We touch here one of the main currents of the Reformation life. However, it was not until men began to emancipate themselves from the glamour of the Calvinistic system as a whole that what we may call free exegesis began. Calvin put men on the way of it, though for a long time he so bound their minds to one particular theology as to make that a conditioning factor of the exegesis.

Lastly, let us emphasize that in all this Calvin's dominant interest was religion. The Scripture is the Word of God for salvation and for no other purpose. This alone gives it its importance. And this alone lies at the back of the mountains of commentaries and exegesis. And all this, as we have seen, was brought down to the level of the common man who everywhere was encouraged to read, mark, learn, and inwardly digest. All the Lord's people must become in a sense exegetes if not prophets. Further, it is the Word itself which engenders faith. Calvin goes even so far as to say, " Take away the Word and no faith will remain " (III.ii.6). This idea linking on with the familiar doctrine that the preaching of the Word is itself a sacrament whereby God comes in grace to the believing heart and enforced by the further idea of the witness of the Spirit, helps to explain the custom that grew up of reading a portion of Scripture daily in the home. The devotional use of the Bible on an extended scale dates from the Reformation and to a large extent rests on Calvinistic theory. Here it may not be pointless to recall that Calvin's own book, the *Institutes*, was written as " an easy introduction " to the sacred

Scriptures to help the believer to " ascertain both what he ought principally to look for in Scripture, and also to what head he ought to refer whatever is contained in it."[1] That it served this purpose for many there is no doubt.

[1] Beveridge, *Inst.* Vol. I, p. 28.

CHAPTER XI

THE PRINCIPLE OF AUTHORITY IN CALVINISM

THE teaching concerning the Scripture which we have just considered does but introduce us to the real problem, namely, that of the seat of authority in religion. Nor do we possess Calvin's full view of the Scripture until we have considered this further point. Alongside the idea of the authority of the Bible he developed his doctrine of the testimony of the Spirit— the *testimonium Spiritus Sancti*. It is generally recognized that this doctrine is the Reformer's special contribution to the difficult problem of authority, that it is indeed a distinctive mark of the Calvinistic theology.

It was Calvin who introduced it with all its implications into dogmatics, but once formulated, it was immediately accepted throughout the whole Protestant world.[1]

Concerning the new principle of authority which all are agreed was proposed by the Reformation it is interesting to note that diverse and indeed totally opposite views have been put forward by different critics. We have already referred to the idea that it merely substituted the Bible for the Pope, thus setting up another purely external authority of the same kind. Over against this it has been maintained

[1] Doumergue: *Op. cit.* Vol. IV, p. 56.   Cf. B. J. Warfield: *Calvin and the Reformation*, p. 209.

in other quarters, that what it really did was to offer a purely subjective authority, making human reason or some sort of intuitive feeling the final arbiter. It established, as is said, the right of private judgment. From both these points of view the Reformation has been discountenanced or commended according to the outlook of the critic. But obviously both views cannot be correct. It can be said in brief that neither view does full justice to Calvin's teaching. Both positions are implicit in that teaching and, as we shall see, both developed from it. There is an emphasis both on the outer and the inner and these obviously can be separated, though in Calvin's thought they are one. For him there is no authority in religion apart from the Bible, but also there is no authority in the Bible apart from the Holy Spirit speaking in the heart. Let one aspect of this view be emphasized to the exclusion of the other and clearly two different, indeed opposite, conceptions arise. And this seems to be what happened.

What then is the doctrine of the testimony of the Spirit?

As we should expect, it rests upon the Reformer's general position. From eternity some are predestinated to salvation, the whole purpose of God in creation being to this end. As we saw at the beginning, the very universe was created for them that they might be saved. In precisely the same way the Bible also exists for their benefit, divinely given and divinely ordained. It is thus the book for the elect. They alone can make anything of it. But, and here is the essential point, the elect can make something of it because they possess in their hearts the witness of the Spirit. This witness both certifies the authority of the Word and gives its correct interpretation. So Scripture bears upon its face for the elect at least, as clear evidence of its truth as white and black do of their colour, sweet and bitter of their taste (I.vii.2). To get benefit from it one must believe it to have come down from heaven as directly as if God had been heard giving utterance to it (I.vii.1). But again this presents no difficulty to the elect who have the inner testimony. Thus all conviction concerning it rests not on human conjectures, judgments, or reasons; the mind with regard to it is formed in the recesses of the soul where the Spirit of God does His work. Secondary arguments relating to the majesty of Scripture, its style and so forth, these it is true can be of use to show that there is a God and that the Law and the Prophets come from Him ; and actually Calvin gives these secondary arguments at some length, evidently feeling that they have a value. But he insists that they can never lead to full faith in Scripture. At best they may establish the Word of God against gainsayers, but they can never give the certainty which faith requires.

With the conviction of the truth of Scripture and of its divine origin there comes also by the agency of the same Spirit the ability to understand and receive the truth. This is equally important. It means that the testimony of the Spirit not only presents the Word as the Word of God, but also gives power to receive it as such, that is, to see its significance for the soul, and to make right use of it in accordance with the purpose for which it was created. The Spirit gives a " new eye " enabling us for the first time to contemplate the heavenly mysteries, and this inner illumination is both the true source of understanding in the intellect, and the great agency in confirming the heart, overcoming both blindness and distrust. These two operations go together as we saw in the discussion of the meaning of faith. The task of confirming the heart according to Calvin is even more difficult than that of enlightening the mind, inasmuch as there is more distrust in the heart than blindness in the mind, and consequently it is more difficult to inspire the soul with security than to imbue it with knowledge (III.ii.35). Thus we see that the problem as it presents itself to the Reformer, is not merely to get a verdict concerning the truth of Scripture, but to get it accepted as the saving Word of God. Of this the Spirit and the Spirit alone is the agent.

The idea underlying the theory is easily seen to be that the one Spirit that created Scripture and brought it forth is present in the heart of the elect to apply it. He who spake by the mouth of the prophets, for example, must penetrate our hearts, in order to convince us that they faithfully delivered the message with which they were divinely entrusted (I.vii.4). Long before Calvin, Athanasius had said that for the proving and true knowledge of the Scriptures there is required the good life and the pure soul and the virtue which is according to Christ.[1] Few would deny this as a general principle. But Calvin is more radical. He is not arguing that for the understanding of any human product there must be as a basis some fellowship of mind with mind, as one might say an artist alone can really appreciate art, or a poet a poem, though the psychology of that fact may perhaps help us to appreciate his point of view. The core of his position however is that here we are not dealing with any human product. In the natural man there is

[1] *De Incarnatione*, c. LVII.

nothing at all that can enable him even to approach it. The Bible is a divine product. It can then be appreciated, read, understood, interpreted, and applied only by a divine gift in the soul. By means of the in-dwelling Spirit alone can that same Spirit's external product be discerned and appropriated. And as that Spirit is the originator of the conversion and spiritual life of the elect, so He and no other is the ground of their attitude to the Scripture. Thus the authority of the Word for the individual is bound up with his conversion and the daily renewal of his spiritual life. The life and the means of life are given and authenticated progressively together.

The following passage from the *Institutes* both expresses the point of view and indicates at the same time something of its significance for the devout mind according to Calvin—" Let it therefore be held as fixed that those who are inwardly taught by the Holy Spirit acquiesce implicitly in Scripture; that Scripture carrying its own evidence along with it, deigns not to submit to proofs and arguments, but owes the full conviction with which we ought to receive it to the testimony of the Spirit. Enlightened by him, we no longer believe, either on our own judgment or that of others, that the Scriptures are from God; but in a way superior to human judgment we feel perfectly assured —as much so as if we beheld the divine image visibly impressed on it—that it came to us by the instrumentality of men, from the very mouth of God. We ask not for proofs or probabilities on which to rest our judgment, but we subject our intellect and judgment to it as too transcendent for us to estimate " (I.vii.5). To this we may add the terse summary of the *Westminster Confession*—" our full persuasion and assurance of the

infallible truth and divine authority thereof is from
the inward work of the Holy Spirit, bearing witness by
and with the Word in our hearts." The last phrase is
important. There is nothing without the Word; there
is equally nothing in the Word without the Spirit.

If the above exposition be carefully considered it
will be seen that while it cannot be simply argued
either that Calvin exalted the Bible to the place of the
Pope, or, on the other hand, established private judgment as against the authority of the Church, yet it
must be admitted that he opened the way for both
developments. After him, as a matter of fact, the
movement went on both lines, and it is interesting and
perhaps significant that on both lines the distinctive
doctrine of the witness of the Spirit tended to recede
into the background. As this happened, in religious
circles the Bible came to be regarded more and more as
a purely external authority, while beyond the distinctive religious sphere, reason came increasingly to be
exalted.

We have already noticed the forces tending to
establish the external authority of the Bible. As we
have seen, Calvin himself never lets that go. It was his
base of operations in his attack both on Rome and on
the subjectivism of the so-called sects. These latter
he opposed not only with vigour but also with abuse—
a sure sign, by the way, that he was not entirely com-
fortable in his logic. It cannot be insisted too
strongly that for him there was no revelation of God
whatever apart from the Bible. As we have noted, the
believer is bound to it on two sides, both for the
knowledge of the truth and for the acceptance of it.
Indeed, Calvin seems to limit the activity of the Holy
Spirit to the Bible just as the Roman Catholic Church

limited it to the Church with its hierarchy and sacraments. In and through the Book the Spirit operates
for the conversion and instruction of men. Further,
Calvin's own example naturally overshadowed his
theory. In all his work the Bible is simply the external
authority so conceived and used. If his immediate
followers took it so, it is only what one would expect.
And it must be admitted that this aspect of the matter
was easier to grasp and to hold than the doctrine of the
witness of the Spirit. It was easier still to use for the
silencing of opponents and the grounding of the dogma.
Not that the idea of the witness of the Spirit ever
dropped out of Calvinism or was ever totally ignored in
the religious circles influenced by the system, but it
came to be so conceived as to be a subordinate factor,
at best reinforcing and establishing in the heart the
authority of the external revelation.

On the other side, if Calvin's position is carefully
examined, it certainly indicates at least the possibility
of an authority essentially inward and really part of
human personality. It is clearly possible to conceive
it as something other than a mere external utterance
before which the individual must bow. Once the Spirit
is given he is the possession of the Christian and, so to
say, part of his personality, nor does the believer
necessarily feel that he accepts the authority of Scripture as something alien, arbitrarily imposed upon him
at the price of his reason. Rather he welcomes it.
There is within him that to which it corresponds. The
acceptance of it is therefore willing and spontaneous. As
Doumergue points out, Calvin here anticipates the
modern theologies which base everything on Christian
experience.[1]

[1] *Op. cit.* p. 60.

Calvin, as we saw in dealing with the results of the Fall, has a decided opinion concerning the utter inability of human reason in the matter of spiritual knowledge. The last thing he wishes to do is to give reason any rights whatever in this sphere. But all the same, whatever his intentions, the doctrine of the inner witness of the Spirit was a step in the direction of that movement which eventually destroyed the external authority both of Bible and Church and substituted for it an authority of the human mind. In this way it broke new ground and looked toward the modern world. It would be too much to expect that Calvin, standing so near the mediaeval outlook, should have wrought out a perfectly coherent conception of an inner spiritual authority, but he undoubtedly pointed the way. Take out from his teaching the distinctively Christian element and it is not really a far step from the inner witness of the Spirit to the " *cogito ergo sum* " of Descartes. The truth would seem to be that many factors were leading in the direction of the new philosophy, and Calvinism, though unwittingly, was one. While it wrought in the common man to establish a new external authority as against the Church of Rome, yet at the same time it influenced the stream of thought which was making in the direction of a further emancipation from the authority of dogma itself. Troeltsch in his *Die Bedeutung des Protestantismus für die Entstehung der modernen Welt* argues that in this respect the sects were the real pioneers of the modern world rather than Lutheranism or Calvinism. They certainly went much further than Calvin in claiming the right of the individual to interpret the Scriptures. That claim ultimately proved to be the solvent of Calvin's position, but all the same, much as the Reformer opposed them, the germ of their view was already present in his teaching. His opposition to Servetus, Castellion, the Anabaptists and the rest only shows that to Calvin himself the position had not been worked out to its logical conclusion. To us these men seem to be claiming much the same right over against him as he himself was claiming over against Rome. His attitude to them and his inability to rise to the idea of toleration shows the measure in which he remained to the end under the dominance of mediaeval trains of thought. And here was the weakness of the theory. It broke new ground, but it stopped short of the final conclusion.

A good illustration of both the difficulty and the strength of the theory is given in an incident in the life of Bunyan. When he was in Bedford gaol a certain Master Cobb was sent to persuade him to be reasonable. Bunyan quoted Scripture. " But," said Master Cobb, " who shall judge between you, for you take the Scripture one way and they another? " Even in Calvin's own day there were those who said the Scripture was like a nose of wax which could be twisted either way.[1] Bunyan gets over the difficulty by admitting that the truth of Scripture has to be arrived at, but maintains that Scripture interprets Scripture.[2] That is, the sense of the whole has to be considered. However, Cobb had put his finger on the place. Can there be different deliverances by the same indwelling Spirit? On the point Calvin himself showed some confusion of thought as we might expect. He seems to have allowed more liberty in the interpreting of Scripture than in the matter of doctrine.[3] His general

[1] Doumergue: *Op. cit.* p. 80.
[2] *A Relation of the Imprisonment of Mr. John Bunyan.*
[3] Tholuck: *Merits of Calvin,* p. 16.

rule for determining the meaning of a doubtful passage was that which accords with faith, faith here being the accepted dogma. But again, whose dogma—his or theirs? Is there not some ground for saying that the Word of God for him was not in reality the Scriptures as such, but his own dogmatic system, which of course he thought to derive from the Scriptures? Yet even on this point in a letter to Archbishop Cranmer concerning the unity of the Church, he expresses the wish that men of learning of the different Churches might get together, and after discussing the different articles of faith, should by a unanimous decision deliver to posterity a certain rule of doctrine.[1] Here the authority looks like the consensus of opinion.

However, all this goes but to show that the Reformer's theory is not logically perfect. Its significance in theology lies in the movements it originated. The doctrine of the witness of the Spirit particularly is an original contribution of permanent value to the discussion of a difficult and vital subject. It has still a place in living theology, which means that it adumbrates a truth which thought cannot easily dispense with. It is interesting to note that it found its way even into Arminian circles. Charles Wesley puts it popularly in the verse

> Come, Holy Ghost, for moved by Thee
> Thy prophets wrote and spoke ;
> Unlock the truth, Thyself the key,
> Unseal the sacred book.

On the other side, Calvinism made it difficult to elaborate a theory of the seat of authority in religion, at least in Christianity, without doing justice to the Bible as the record of a real revelation. The modern insistence

[1] Schaff: *Op. cit.* p. 799.

on the fact that Christianity is a historical religion and therefore closely bound up with its documents, owes not a little to the place which Calvinism succeeded in securing for the Bible in the minds of Christian men. The whole matter is well summed up by Mackintosh in the following passage—" It is misleading to say that the secret and inspiration of the new evangelical message was the right of private judgment, which is in no sense a distinctively religious idea; nor is this secret to be found either in the affirmation of the immediate access of the soul to God, which can hardly be denied to great saints like St. Bernard. Actually it lay in a new thought of the intrinsic authority belonging to God's revelation of Himself. It was the discovery that unless Jesus Christ attests Himself to the soul in whom His Word has been made living and powerful by the Holy Spirit, the Christian religion cannot be made to live. In consequence the Reformers taught that, the believer being face to face with God, his convictions are reached by responsible decision, in the spontaneous act of faith. They are the Spirit-prompted response of his mind and heart to the Word. They are convictions which God leaves him no option but to hold . . . a new principle for theology had been introduced, viz., that truth revealed in Christ admits of no external proof, but is made the inward possession of the believing mind by the convincing power of the Holy Spirit."[1]

[1] H. R. Mackintosh: *Types of Modern Theology*, pp. 6-7.

Chapter XII

THE CALVINISTIC WAY OF LIFE

CALVINISM from the beginning has everywhere meant a clearly defined attitude to life. Historically, as we have already seen, this has been as fruitful as the dogmatic system on which it rests, and even after the theology was to some extent abandoned the life-discipline had a tendency to remain. It is surely not the smallest merit of the movement that it succeeded in impressing upon thousands its peculiar ethical ideals and aims, even bringing whole peoples into subjection to them. So that the typical Calvinist in both the new and the old world stands out as a man of quite distinct ethical outlook.

In this respect Calvin has sometimes been compared, not unjustly, with Ignatius Loyola. His chapters on the Life of the Christian were indeed published separately and for many people served as the equivalent of the *Spiritual Exercises*. Both men built on the idea of self-discipline under God, and both wanted this in the service of a vigorous and ceaseless activity on behalf of God in the world. Except that, while the founder of the Jesuits organized only a society under discipline, Calvin succeeded with a very large number of ordinary people. Also in Calvinism the discipline applied in the ordinary avocations of life. It was not a cloistered virtue, nor on the other hand was it for certain special tasks only. It was a discipline to enable men to live day by day, and ordinary daily life was to be the expression of it. Indeed, this organizing of the whole of a man's life under one comprehensive dominant idea is one of the chief features of Calvinism. It supplied a great, and what proved to be for a long time very effective, ethical motive—one that the common man could grasp and to a remarkable degree use. If it is legitimate to ask why one ought to live the good life, Calvin gave on the point a concise answer.

The motive is, as is well known, the promotion of the glory of God. This according to Calvin is the " universal rule " by which a Christian man must regulate his conduct. " The great point," he says, " is that we who are consecrated and dedicated to God should not henceforth think or speak, design or act without a view to His glory " (III.vii.1). No part of life whatever is to be exempt from this injunction. Rather all is to be organized with this end in view. Not that evangelical perfection is to be so strictly insisted on as to make us refuse to acknowledge as Christian any man who has not attained it, but this should be regarded always as the goal towards which we should run (III.vi.5).

The real significance of such an idea of the motive of action is that it puts God in the centre of thought rather than man. Life is to be regulated with reference to its author to whom it belongs. At no other point perhaps is Calvinism more clearly separated from the prevailing sentiment of our own time. Since the evangelical revival of the eighteenth century and the romanticism of Rousseau, ethics have been regarded largely from the point of view of human good, either the good of the individual or the reorganization of society as a whole. The goal has been to promote human happiness and the appeal leading to action has been largely to obvious human need and to the sympathy which is evoked by it. Thus man's requirements

o

in this world to a large extent determined the content
of so-called ethical action, which content has with the
years become increasingly concerned with purely
material blessings.   In a word it has been an age
dominated by humanitarianism.   It would, of course,
be absurd to suggest that Calvin had no place in his
system for such humane sentiments, but the important
point is that with him they are not primary.   He maintains that no man can do good for its own sake apart
from God and the reference to God.   The one adequate
motive and the pure motive is the doing of God's will
because it is His will (III.vii.2).   When Macaulay
says—" The Puritan hated bear-baiting not because it
gave pain to the bear, but because it gave pleasure to
the spectators "[1], he completely misreads Puritanism
in the second part of his sentence, but he uttered more
than a half-truth in the first.   The actual motive of the
true Calvinist in all such protests was not pity for the
bear, or for that matter sympathy with oppressed
human beings; it was a strenuous opposition to something that was contrary to the will of God and unworthy of men created in the divine image.   It is just
this aspect of Calvinism which makes it appear a severe,
stern system in an age such as ours which has lost all
vision of any other motive than the purely humanitarian.   At the same time it was just this element of
Calvinism that gave strength of character and rigidity
of will, with its freedom from feeble sentimentalism.
Central in the system is neither the happiness of
the individual nor the good of society, but the doing
of the will of God for His glory.   The religious life
is the true life, and the religious life is by definition
the life that is lived with reference to God.   Such

[1] *History of England*, Vol. I, p. 161.

reference to God is prior to any reference to human need.

This idea of promoting the glory of God was linked on to the idea that all life here is a preparation for the life beyond. The Christian has to be perfected for his destiny. He is so perfected not by doing some special service in addition to his normal work, but by making his whole life subject to the divine will. He is thus called upon to devote his whole energy of mind to the service of God (III.vii.1). Life has one stern purpose to which there must be complete devotion. The end of the calling determines the stages of the preparation.

The content of the ethic is unfolded as this idea is developed. The calling demands the renunciation of self or, to use Calvin's own term, self-denial. This means literally the denying of the self, and in the first instance the denial of the right of reason to rule and regulate the life. Where philosophy tells us to follow reason, Christianity urges complete submission to the Holy Spirit. Thus the ethical life presupposes conversion. It is possible only as the result of the saving activity within. The thought is not that a man must deny himself in order that he may become religious, but rather that being now religious he is able to live the life. By denying himself he gradually becomes conformed to the image of the Saviour.

This self-denial is not merely renunciation. Rather it has at every point positive value. When rightly understood, it relates partly to our neighbour and partly to God. It is the laying aside of all private regard for ourselves in such a way as to divest the mind of all excessive longing for wealth, power or human favour and to leave no place for pride, show, or ostentation, or avarice, lust, luxury and effeminacy, or indeed

any of the vices which are engendered by self-love
(III.vii.2). On the other side it is the giving of oneself
fully to God and one's neighbour. In and through it
the believer becomes the instrument of the divine will
and so approximates to the divine character.

In dealing with the aspect of it that relates to one's
neighbour Calvin develops his well-known doctrine of
stewardship, a doctrine the more remarkable, because,
as indicated above, it is based on other foundation than
that of pity. First, we are not to envy those who
possess more than we ourselves possess, but rather to
honour them as being honoured of God with such
possessions. This makes us courteous and friendly
(III.vii.4). Then with regard to everything that God
has bestowed upon us and by which we can aid our
neighbour we are to consider ourselves His stewards
and are bound to give an account of our stewardship.
All the endowments we possess are " divine deposits "
to be used for His glory (III.vii.5). Further, we are
enjoined to do good to all without exception, even
though they may be unworthy of it if estimated by
their own merit. Scripture enjoins a most excellent
reason for this when it tells us that we are not to look
to what men deserve in themselves, but to attend to
the image of God, which exists in all, and to which we
owe honour and love. To this idea Calvin devotes a
page (III.vii.6). It is an idea which admirably illustrates how his motive of promoting the glory of God
can operate in daily life and also how such a motive
cuts deeper into life than mere humanitarian sentiment.
However, the Reformer urges that sympathy must not
be lacking. It is not enough for the Christian " to carry
cheerfulness in his looks " and to give attractiveness to
the discharge of his duties by courteous language. All

must be done out of " a pure feeling of love " (III.vii.7).
The Christian must exercise his imagination in order
truly to feel the need which he is endeavouring to
relieve. Here we have no mean conception of ministry
in daily life, and moreover, ministry with and through
the normal endowments of personality. It comes in
the way of one's calling.

Then, secondly, self-denial has reference to God.
This consists chiefly in resigning ourselves to Him in
the present life. On the one hand the natural man
tends to pursue wealth, to intrigue for power, and to
collect the frivolities which seem conducive to luxury
and splendour, on the other hand he has a dread of
poverty, mean birth, and a humble condition, and feels
the strongest desire to guard against them. This leads
to restlessness and all sorts of wiles and entanglements.
The Christian avoids such perils by hoping for and
longing for no prosperity apart from the blessing of
God. Such blessing alone can bring true happiness,
and on it the Christian can and must confidently rely.
Also by it a curb is put on all wrong ambition and such
acts as injure our neighbour. Further, the Christian is
taught by it to bear his humble lot with endurance and
patience, while in it is the secret of tranquillity and
endurance amid all the accidents and pains of mortal
life. Whatever happens he will not cease to bless the
Lord. " He alone has properly denied himself, who
has resigned himself entirely to the Lord, placing all
the course of his life at His disposal " (III.vii.8).

With this there is the bearing of the cross. " Those
whom the Lord has chosen and honoured with His
intercourse must prepare for a hard, laborious, troubled
life, a life full of many and various kinds of evils "
(III.viii.1). Calvin does not hesitate to say that it is

the Father's will to exercise His people by thus putting them to the proof. Christ himself had to bear his cross in order to testify and prove his obedience to the Father. So the Christian is visited with disgrace or poverty or bereavement or disease and other afflictions in order to teach him his frailty and lead him to cast himself before God. Even the best of men need to be led to a more thorough knowledge of themselves by this kind of trial. It makes for progress in humility and for the destruction of all confidence in the flesh. It is a necessary training in obedience.

Here we have again Calvin's characteristic note. He offers not merely a counsel of endurance or a philosophy of suffering. Rather he gives suffering itself a positive value in the scheme of life so that one might even come to welcome it as a help toward perfection. His phrase is " willingly and cheerfully receive it " (III.viii.8). Thus everything that can come in life, whether wealth or poverty, success or failure, joy or sorrow, everything is part of the discipline of life and a further opportunity of showing forth God's glory.

A special application of this aspect of the teaching lies in the duty of bearing persecution for righteousness' sake. This includes striving for the defence of the Gospel and for righteousness in every place. It may involve poverty, exile, contempt, imprisonment, ignominy and even death itself. " But when the favour of God breathes upon us there is none of these things which may not turn to our own happiness. . . . If while conscious of our innocence we are deprived of our substance by the wickedness of man, we are, no doubt, humanly speaking, reduced to poverty, but in truth, our riches in heaven are increased; if driven from our homes, we have a more welcome reception into the family of God; if vexed or despised, we are more firmly rooted in Christ; if stigmatized by disgrace and ignominy, we have a higher place in the kingdom of God; if we are slain, entrance is thereby given to us to eternal life. The Lord, having set such a price on us, let us be ashamed to estimate ourselves at less than the shadowy and evanescent allurements of the present life " (III. viii.7).

However, while the Christian is to face this conflict not without the natural feeling of pain, he is not to have his feelings blunted according to the iron philosophy of Stoicism, nor to agree with the " new kind of Stoics amongst Christians who hold it vicious not only to groan and weep but even to be sad and anxious " (III. viii.8).

These observations the Reformer makes, he says, to keep pious minds from despair and from finding it impossible to divest themselves of the natural feeling of grief. This would be to convert patience into stupor and a brave and firm man into a block. In affliction we shall groan and be discouraged and so on, but the consolation will be that " the Lord has so willed." The end will be " cheerfully to endure," knowing that in the very cross with which the Father afflicts us He provides for our salvation. Hence arises thanksgiving even in the midst of sufferings.

That this doctrine had very great effect is proved by the history of Calvinism. We have here the teaching that produced and sustained the " Church under the Cross." That it nerved men for high endeavour as well as enabled them to persevere in spite of insuperable obstacles none will doubt. It was in Calvinistic circles the antidote to all defeatism. Its strength was partly in the belief in the inflexible will of God, and partly in the attitude of strenuous activity which it inculcated in all circumstances, demanding a vigorous and not a passive attitude of mind even in the midst of extreme bodily weakness. Psychologically this exaltation of mind over body was one of the strong points of the Calvinistic discipline. It not only taught men to dare and to do, but also to suffer. By lifting suffering itself into the realm of service it sought to make the Christian invulnerable in all circumstances, even the most sinister, by reason of his faith in God.

> They also serve who only stand and wait.

Milton, indeed, admirably expressed the spirit of the Calvinistic ethics both in his poetry and his life. Having arrived at the age of twenty-three, he considers his life from the point of view of its fruitfulness and resolves to live " as ever in my great taskmaster's eye "; while both in the sonnet just quoted " *On his blindness* " and in the reference to the same calamity in the opening lines of the third book of *Paradise Lost*, he refuses to allow any slackening of effort, or to find in it any excuse for failure, and the very word he uses is Calvin's great word—" patience."

> Patience to prevent that murmur soon replies.

His grief at his blindness is real, but his victory over it is complete.

Add to all this Calvin's further chapter (III.ix) on the value of meditating on the future life as a help to endurance in this life and you have then all the elements of the New England outlook.

> Life is real, life is earnest,
> And the grave is not its goal.

A comparison of Longfellow's *Psalm of Life* with

Henley's Stoic hymn " I am the master of my fate, I am the captain of my soul " brings out well the similarity of the two systems as also the difference in atmosphere between them. The attitude is that of the soldier facing all odds but sustaining a long campaign and triumphing at last through patience and endurance. But while Stoicism relies on the essential qualities of man regarded as self-sufficient for all tasks, Calvinism makes man strong through his faith in God, and especially in God's firm control of every detail of the situation. For Stoic fate we have Calvinistic predestination, and in place of man's ability, the irresistible power and will of Almighty God. Calvinism was not a whit behind Stoicism in inculcating fortitude, but in addition it had the dynamic of faith in the living God, a faith possible even to the common man. It was thus no aristocratic ethic but a system of life which could be made to run in the highways and byways of the work-a-day world.

Chapter XIII

CALVINISM AND THE SOCIAL ORDER

IN addition to the teaching on self-denial indicated in the last chapter, Calvin also has a teaching about the use of the world and its goods, which had great significance for the Calvinistic social life. The ethic is at one and the same time both the renunciation of the world and its dominance. On the one hand the Reformer can use the most pessimistic statements about this life, saying it is nothing but misery, a place of exile, a sepulchre and prison (III.ix.4), yet on the other side the general effect of his teaching was to stimulate an active and aggressive temper which tended to subordinate all material goods to the control of the believer. It is this factor which gives the peculiar flavour to what modern writers have called the asceticism of Calvinism as against, say, that of Luther. While Lutheranism tolerates the world Calvin sent out his followers to master it.

The contempt he argues which believers should train themselves to feel for the present life must not be of a kind to beget hatred of it or ingratitude to God for it. Though abounding in all kinds of wretchedness, yet this life is justly classed among divine blessings which are not to be despised. Unless we recognize the goodness of God in it we are chargeable with no little ingratitude towards Him. Indeed, before openly exhibiting the inheritance of eternal glory God is pleased to manifest Himself to us as Father by minor proofs, viz., the blessings which He bestows upon us here, so that even this life serves to acquaint us with His goodness. Hence, however true it may be that death is the gateway to eternal bliss, this life itself is a good for which we must give thanks, and which is in various ways " a foretaste of the divine benignity " (III.ix.3). Nor is there any doubt that in this life we can have such a foretaste.

Since, therefore, we are intended to live we are bound to use the necessary supports of life, nor can we shun without incurring blame even those things which seem more subservient to delight than to necessity (III.x.1). The rule is to observe a mean. We can use them all with a pure conscience both for necessity and pleasure, so long as we use them in such a way that they further rather than retard our progress. The counsel of some that we should avoid all abuse by using corporeal goods only so far as they are necessaries, Calvin describes as " unnecessarily austere " (III.x.1). It binds consciences closer than does the Word of God. Some maintain that it ought to be left to individual consciences, but Calvin holds that while on the one hand consciences cannot be bound by fixed and definite laws, Scripture, on the other hand, has laid down general rules which are sufficient, and it is necessary to keep within the limits which they prescribe.

We shall not go far astray if we consider and keep in mind the end for which these things were created. Food, for example, is both for necessity and for delight, so also clothing, herbs, fruits, trees, etc. Were it not so, the prophet would not enumerate among the mercies of God " wine that maketh glad the heart of man and oil to make his face to shine " (Ps. civ. 15). Even the natural qualities of things demonstrate to what end and how far they may be lawfully enjoyed—flowers to

please the eye, odours to delight the sense of smell,
qualities in gold and silver and ivory to make them
precious above other metals and stones. The use of
these things is permitted, nay rather ordained by
divine providence; nor was it ever forbidden to laugh,
to be full, or to add new to old and hereditary possessions, or to be delighted with music or to drink wine
(III.xix.9). In short God has given many things a
value without any necessary use, and He wills us to
rejoice through our senses. Then says Calvin, " Have
done with that inhuman philosophy which in allowing
no use of the creatures but for necessity, not only
maliciously deprives us of the lawful fruit of the divine
beneficence, but cannot be realized without depriving
man of his senses, and reducing him to a block "
(III.x.3). In passing it may be noted that the Reformer himself was not without his sober enjoyments,
being in reality far removed from the sombre morose
individual pictured by later caricature.[1]

In all this there is clearly quite a different tone from
that of the old asceticism with its utter contempt for
the things of time and sense. Calvin deliberately takes
up the world and all that therein is into his theological
and ethical scheme. It is God's world, created by Him
for the proper use and training of man. The creature is
to be quite clearly distinguished from the creator and
all idolatry avoided. But the creature always has the
merit of having been created by God, and God's works
must not be despised by neglect of use.

Care must be taken, however, against the lusts of the
flesh which tend to all manner of licence. Since the
one object of creating all things was to teach men to
know their author, where is the gratitude if they so

[1] J. Mackinnon : *op. cit.* p. 275.

gorge and stultify themselves with feasting and wine
as to be unfit for the offices of piety or the duties of their
calling? Where the recognition of God, if the flesh,
boiling over in lust through excessive indulgence, infects
the mind with its impurity, so as to lose the discernment of honour and rectitude? Where thankfulness to
God for clothing, if on account of sumptuous raiment
we both admire ourselves and disdain others? . . . For
many are so devoted to luxury in all their senses that
their mind lies buried. Many are so delighted with
marble, gold, and pictures, that they become marble-
hearted—are changed as it were into metal and made
like painted figures (III.x.3).

The principle is that all things are to be used in such
a way as to contribute to health of body and mind so
that we may thereby serve God and do good. The
three rules which Scripture lays down for the right
use of worldly goods are, first, the despising of this
life and aspiring to celestial immortality; then the
bearing of poverty patiently and without shame; and
lastly the offices of charity which demand stewardship.

Finally life is regulated by one's " calling." God has
assigned distinct duties to each and none may presume
to overstep his proper limits. Every man's mode of
life is a sort of station assigned him by the Lord that
he may not always be driven about at random. This
to counteract the boiling restlessness of the human
mind, the fickleness with which it is borne hither and
thither and its inordinate ambition. In all circumstances the recognition of this call of the Lord is the
beginning and foundation of right action, and he who
fails to act with reference to it will not keep the right
path. Hence he who directs his life to this end will
have it properly framed, nor will he attempt more than

his calling justifies. And everyone, from magistrate to the father of a family, will bear the inconvenience of his calling, its cares, uneasiness, and anxiety, persuaded that God and no other has laid the burden on him. No work will be so mean and sordid as not to have value and splendour in the eye of God (III.x.6). Here we have the exalting of daily work, every detail of life being given a potential religious significance.

These then are the two sides of Calvin's ethical teaching. First the systematic self-denial applying to the whole of life, and secondly, the permission to use the good things of life in accordance with the intention of their creator. The crucial points in it are the devout acceptance of the facts of life and one's environment, all stations being by divine appointment; the refusal altogether to succumb to the environment however trying; the idea of calling abolishing the sharp distinction between secular and sacred and making all work an opportunity of glorifying God; the duty of living in all details according to the Gospel; and lastly the duty of glorifying God also in the right use of material possessions. Obviously underlying such an ethic there is a spirit of strenuous activity. Men are encouraged to live, sent out to live. They are to master the world, dominate it, bend it indeed to their supreme religious aim. Thus, as Weber points out, the old asceticism was transformed, it was no longer confined to a cell or a society, but was to be a vigorous activity *within* the world, every Christian to be, as it were, a monk all the days of his life.[1]

The same writer with others sees in this forceful ethic the religious basis of Capitalism. Some have even gone so far as to claim that Capitalism is indeed the

[1] M. Weber: *The Protestant Ethic and the spirit of Capitalism*, p. 120.

secular descendant of Calvinism. " The immense economic advance of the nineteenth century," writes Sir
Josiah Stamp, " was the joint product of Calvin and
James Watt. Their departed spirits worked in unconscious partnership to make the greatest business
concern the world has ever known."[1] Certain it is that
the two things grew together. Calvinists from early
days became the pioneers in trade and industry,
many of them both in England and America being
obliged to enter these spheres because others were
closed to them. Thus the Calvinistic countries became
the countries where the capitalistic system developed.
" Wherever you have active Calvinism in the past,"
writes Mr. Hilaire Belloc, " wherever you have the air
of Calvinism surviving to-day, there you have mercantile order, mercantile adventure, mercantile foresight,
mercantile success; and such order and foresight and
the rest are even more developed on the side of finance
than on the side of commerce. It is the story of New
England, it is the story of Scotland, it is the story of
Geneva, it is the story of the French Huguenots."[2]
He goes on to argue that it is the possession of liquid
wealth which gives families still dominantly Huguenot
their power in modern French capitalism. Thus
Calvinism and Capitalism are historically related.

Apart from the main underlying principles of the
Calvinistic ethics which we have already made clear,
there are one or two other factors which help to
elucidate the connection between them. First, it
was fateful that Calvin, under the influence of the
Old Testament one would think, threw his blessing

[1] Stamp : *Motive and Method in a Christian Order*, p. 114. Cf.
K. S. Latourette: *History of the Expansion of Christianity*, Vol. III,
pp. 407-8.
[2] *Monarchy*, p. 310.

over the possession of wealth. Since God gives it and
ordains its possession, the idea readily emerges that it
is a mark of God's favour. As such it can be received
and rejoiced in, and indeed must not lightly be abandoned by the individual, since it is a solemn trust from
the Almighty. Further, it is the reward of labour, and
Calvinism honoured labour and frowned on idleness.
Indeed, for the first time ordinary daily work was taken
up into the religious sphere and made the right, normal
activity of all good men. Since idleness is sinful, all
are to make the most of their talents, and to value the
reward which labour brings. Then the idea of stewardship demanded the same thoughtfulness and care in
the spending of money as in the getting of it. The
outlook condemned all wasteful expenditure. Thus the
outcome of it was that, if it invested the rich man with
serious responsibilities, it still allowed him to be rich,
and indeed, rich according to his station. In this it
saw nothing unchristian. Rather it gave an emphatic
sanction.

Secondly, Calvin came down firmly on the side of
private property. This again is God's ordering and the
distinctions of social status which it implies are part of
the permanent structure of society. Such reasoning
was traced back to the Decalogue. In treating of the
eighth commandment, *Thou shalt not steal*, the Reformer writes, " For we must consider that what each
individual possess has not fallen to him by chance,
but by the distribution of the Sovereign Lord of all,
that no one can pervert his means to bad purposes
without committing a fraud on a divine dispensation "
(II.viii.44). Elsewhere he argues that the possession of
private property is necessary for the peace of society
(III.iv.12) and urges that we are to lend our counsel

and aid to assist men to retain it (II.viii.46). Nor was such teaching a dead letter in Calvinism, witness the *Christian Directory* of Baxter and the general attitude of Calvinists and those under the influence of the system even to the present day. There is here a veritable tenacity concerning private property. No doubt in early days the excesses of Anabaptists and Levellers led to some emphasis on the point, but the real root of the attitude is this idea of divine providence with its distribution of gifts. That is to say, in Calvinism, property shelters under the protection of a religious idea, and moreover, that religious idea which is fundamental in the theology, namely, the inscrutable, but nevertheless unimpeachable will of God. Thus if Calvinism did something to destroy the divine right of kings it did much to put in its place the doctrine of the divine right of property, and the significance of this fact just at the time when the movement of life was toward trade expansion and commerce, and away from the old agrarian organization, can hardly be over-estimated.

Thirdly, Calvin accepted the principle of usury which perhaps more than any other factor made modern capitalism possible. In doing so he was rejecting mediaeval Canon Law but at the same time only following the practice that had become common. As against feudalism he recognized the legitimacy of production on a money basis, with credit as a necessity to it. In his activities at Geneva he shows a real interest in this side of life. Many of his letters deal with questions of finance, trade and industry. We have noted earlier his work in connexion with the starting of the silk industry in the city. He co-operated in other ways with the State in its economic problems,

P

and his successors followed in the same path, advising
the State, fixing rates of interest, making regulations
for controlling such matters, establishing a State Bank
and so forth. However, only credit for business was
allowed, not " usury credit " merely for living on
interest. That is, the usury was for work and not for
idleness. Also from poor men no interest was to be
taken, and the rate of interest on all borrowings was
not to exceed a certain maximum legally fixed according to the needs of the situation. Troeltsch, who
mentions these details, says of Calvinism, " It is the
only form of Christian social doctrine which accepts
the basis of the modern economic situation without
reserve."[1]

Lastly, the strong sense of organization in Calvinism
undoubtedly prepared the way for the later development of the gathering and the use of blocks of capital
by a group or company. The guinea subscription for
religious and charitable purposes became very common
in the seventeenth century, and from this it was an
easy step to the organization of capital on a large scale
for the purposes of industry.

Such then are the factors which further elucidate the
Calvinistic system of ethics and which bring us nearer
to the well-known type of Christian business men in
both Great Britain and America. It would probably
be going too far to say that Calvinism produced
Capitalism without adding important qualifications to
the statement. It would seem truer to argue with
Professor Tawney that Calvinism was only one of the
factors in the wide development leading to the rise of
Capitalism.[2] That some form of Capitalism would
have come without Calvinism seems a reasonable

[1] Troeltsch: *Op. cit.* p. 647.   [2] *Religion and the Rise of Capitalism.*

assumption, but history records that just at the time when Capitalism was about to move forward to its strength, there was found ready in the world a religious outlook and system of ethics which admirably suited it and naturally furthered it. True it is that for good or ill Calvinism helped to mould a new social order and was itself in turn moulded by it. It may not be far wrong to say that as the Roman Catholic Church of the Middle Ages was the Church fitted to the age of feudalism, so Calvinism was the Church adapted to the needs of a rising civilization built on capitalistic lines. Troeltsch utters an impressive verdict in the following passage, " Along with the organic and patriarchal fundamental theory of the mediaeval idea of society, Calvinism has become the second great Christian definite social ideal of European society. . . . Indeed, the great importance of the Calvinistic social theory does not consist merely in the fact that it is one type of Christian social doctrine; its significance is due to the fact that it is one of the great types of sociological thought in general. In inner significance and historical power the types of the French optimistic equalitarian democracy, of State Socialism, of proletarian Communist Socialism, and of the mere theory of power, are, in comparison with Calvinism, far behind."[1]

It is sometimes brought as a charge against Calvinism that it was blind to the evils of Capitalism if it did not actually produce them. That it did not see the whole of the development is, of course, a truism. A just estimate of its responsibility for ,the evils of modern society would have to take account of the fact that those evils have become serious as the original spirit of Calvinism has died away. It ought not to be

[1] *Op. cit.* p. 621.

forgotten that in Calvinism at its zenith there was a deep
religious earnestness and a high sense of responsibility.
Nor can it be denied that Calvinism made this operative
in the secular life of the world. The doctrine of
stewardship was by no means a dead letter, nor did
Calvinism itself know anything of an aggressiveness
unchecked by strong religious and moral considerations. Excessive interest was denounced as sin to be
punished, in the early days at least, by ecclesiastical
as well as civil penalties. Baxter holds that it is a false
rule to sell at the price one can get. He refused to
sanction the sacrifice of moral considerations to the
tender mercies of the law of supply and demand. For
a long time the idea of a fair price with a just reward
for labour ruled. Nor is it right to saddle Calvinism
with the more recent excesses of Capitalism since the
day when the impersonal company usurped the place
of the intimate contact of master and man. A full
study of the subject would have to take into its pur-
view the changes in the Capitalistic system itself. The
two gravest faults of the Puritan outlook, according to
Professor H. G. Wood,[1] are that it failed to reach any
clear conception of the indebtedness of the rich to the
poor, that is, an adequate conception of the real
structure of society, and secondly, that it did not press
any strong criticism of ownership. These are serious
defects, but over against them we have to stress the
moral earnestness and the high sense of responsibility
which actuated the many who came under the influence
of the teaching. When all is said, it remains a fact that
Calvinism exerted a powerful and vitalizing influence
on society. Its influence was mixed but in the mixture

---

[1] *Property—its Duties and Rights*, by various writers (Macmillan
and Co.), pp. 162-3.

there was good.   Gratitude to this now much-abused
social order of the nineteenth century is overdue,
writes Sir Josiah Stamp.[1] In such gratitude, when it
is paid, Calvinism will have its share.

[1] *Op. cit.* p. 114.

Chapter XIV

CHURCH AND STATE

THE Calvinistic conception of the relationship of Church and State is not easy to elucidate owing to the fact that thought on the matter developed under the influence of varying political circumstances. Even the later editions of the *Institutes* show a more radical position than the earlier, while the immediate followers of the Reformer went further still. Considering the subject as a whole we may say that the teaching on the one hand produced a ferment of democratic ideas, while on the other it wrought in a conservative direction towards the support of established authority. The germs of both tendencies lie in the system.

With Calvin as already seen, the important thing is the holy community. This as far as possible has to be realized on earth. Its realization thus becomes the goal of all human endeavour, and all arrangements ordained of God are for this purpose. Thus both Church and State are united in one object. The aim is to produce a worthy Christian civilization, a model society, with uniformity of faith; and for the accomplishment of this purpose Church and State are thought of together, with a tendency almost to regard them as one. Hence it comes about that Calvinism always concerns itself with the State, makes demands on the State in the name of God and religion, and is ever ready to offer advice to the State. At a later time in England and America particularly, it came under the influence of that type of thinking which sought to solve the problem by carefully differentiating the functions of the two partners of civilization and as far as possible avoiding conflict. But it should be noted that in reality this point of view is not the logical outcome of the Calvinistic position. Calvinism claims the State in a much more emphatic way than do the rest of the Free Churches, or, for that matter, than Lutheranism. The State not less than the Church is also an instrument in the hand of God even though its allotted task is different.

Thus the State has an enduring place in society and all the prestige which belongs to a divine ordinance Calvin in treating of the matter takes the statements in the New Testament concerning obedience to rulers and so on at their face value, and also finds support in the more theocratic sections of the Old Testament. He starts out with the idea of two appointed governments for man, the one placed in the soul and inward, relating to eternal life, the other that which has to do with civil institutions and the external regulation of manners (IV.xx.1). This latter he insists is necessary if only because there are things to do which the Church itself cannot undertake. The union of Church and State can be achieved, but only as men avoid extremes.

Some there are who hearing that liberty is praised in the gospel think that they can receive no benefit from the gospel as long as they see any power whatever placed over them. Hence they would change the whole world till there shall be neither courts, laws nor magistrates. Others again are for extolling the power of princes above measure opposing it even to the government of God (IV.xx.1). Here the Reformer clearly has in view the opposing tendencies of his time, and as against the anarchical tendencies he takes a firm stand as indeed did all the reformers. He is on the side of stable government. " Wherefore no man can doubt that civil authority is, in the sight of God, not only sacred and lawful, but the most sacred and by far the most honourable of all stations in mortal life " (IV.xx. 4). So rulers are " vicegerents of God " and must exhibit themselves as a kind of image of divine providence, guardianship, goodness, benevolence and justice (IV.xx.6). God Himself is present and also presides in enacting laws and exercising judicial enquiry (IV.xx.4). The magistrate, in inflicting punishment, acts not of himself but executes the very judgments of God (IV.xx.10). Taken by itself, all this constitutes a doctrine of the State as rigorous as any absolutist could desire, and for a religious man it could mean little less than blind obedience.

However, it is modified by the function of the State as Calvin sees it. Piety must be its first care, and those laws are absurd which disregard the rights of God and consult only for men (IV.xx.9). The business of the State is " to foster and maintain the external worship of God, to defend sound doctrine and the condition of the Church, to adapt our conduct to human society, to form our manners to civil justice, to conciliate us to each other, to cherish common peace and tranquillity " (IV.xx.2). In another passage the Reformer says, " Its object is not merely to enable men to breathe, eat, drink and be warmed (though it certainly includes all these, while it enables them to live together) this, I say, is not its only object, but it is that no idolatry, no blasphemy against the name of God, no calumnies against His truth, nor other offences to religion, break out and be disseminated against the people; that the public quiet be not disturbed, that every man's property be kept secure, that men may carry on innocent commerce with each other, that honesty and modesty be cultivated; in short, that a public form of religion may exist among Christians, and humanity amongst men " (IV.xx.3).

Primarily, therefore, the function of the State is to establish and maintain an order of society in which the Church can exist and do its necessary work. Further, it must use its authority and force to enable the Church to exist even to the extent of acting as the Church's servant in the matter of making laws and enforcing discipline. Thus the Church becomes the monitress of the State, teaching it its purpose, advising it concerning its way, and in turn giving it full assistance in the performing of its task. Thus they mutually support each other, but the Church is supreme. Or to put it another way, the State, like all human beings and every institution, comes under the divine discipline of which the Church is the guardian and the teacher. All is under God, but since the Church possesses the revelation of the will of God and is pre-eminently His chosen instrument for promoting His glory on earth, clearly she has the duty also of oversight over the State. Thus the theory makes in the direction of a real power of control. And however difficult it was for Calvinism in the different countries to which it spread to achieve anything like full control, yet this purpose remained in its consciousness and determined in many ways its policy. It stood always for something more than the spiritual autonomy of the Church over against the State. It visualized the co-partnership in such a way as left it no option but to concern itself with the question of government and to seek persistently the kind of government which would whole-

heartedly support its aim. It is this fact which explains
the opposition of the Huguenots and then the English
Presbyterians to absolute monarchy, not indeed absolute monarchy as such, but the actual monarchy which
was preventing the preaching of the gospel and steadily
refusing to promote the glory of God on earth in the
Calvinistic way. Thus the opposition was mainly in
the interests of the Church and only indirectly for the
good of man. The same fact elucidates the development of the colonies of America, where, as we have
seen, government and religion were closely allied. In
Geneva and, to a less degree, in Scotland, the theocratic
idea was more fully realized.

There were two considerations in the early days
tending to drive Calvinists towards more democratic
theories. First the persecutions in France, England
and Scotland, which brought men there face to face
with absolute monarchy, and secondly the example of
Geneva. Calvin himself seems to have started with
the idea that the actual form of government was a
matter of indifference. He even suggests that it is an
altogether idle occupation for private citizens to
discuss the question at all, divine providence having
arranged for different countries to be governed by
different forms of polity. The wish to change is both
foolish and pernicious (IV.xx.8). Later, however, he
gave some countenance to the republican form as it
existed at Geneva. It is safer and more tolerable, he
says, when several bear rule, one curbing the excess of
another. He calls it an aristocracy bordering on
popular government. " And as I willingly admit,"
he writes, " there is no kind of government happier
than where liberty is framed with becoming moder-
ation and duly constituted so as to be durable, so I

deem those very happy who are permitted to enjoy that form, and I admit that they do nothing at variance with their duty when they strenuously and constantly labour to preserve and maintain it " (IV.xx.8). The procedure at Geneva shows that against such a form of government the Reformer would allow no opposition either civil or religious.

Here then was an alternative theory for Calvinism to oppose against that of absolute monarchy. But also it was a theory that in many ways fitted in with the general outlook of the new religion. This brought, as we have noticed, in more ways than one the emancipation of the common man. Even the Church theory itself was based on the rights of the individual; he could approach God direct through the merits of the mediator, in the Church he was called upon to collaborate with his fellows in the work of government and administration, to exercise his vote with full consciousness of responsibility, to take his share when called upon in public duty, and he was trained to exercise a sort of supervision, not to say criticism, over those in office. All this was an admirable political training and made it difficult for Calvinists to be indifferent to the form of government under which they lived. Troeltsch holds that even at Geneva the ultimate appeal of Calvin and his successors was to the people as the actual sovereign authority.[1] It is not surprising, therefore, that in many ways the system stimulated thought on democratic lines and in the time of persecution tended towards republicanism.

This more radical movement was aided further by the clear enunciation of the right of rebellion, the

[1] *Op. cit.* pp. 628-9.

point at which politically Calvinism diverged most
definitely from mediaeval feudalism. Calvin's own
words could easily be taken in this sense, and in face
of such an event as the massacre of St. Bartholomew
were so taken by Beza and others. Quite an extensive
literature grew up in which the sovereign right of the
people as such was ardently propagated. The best
known of these writers, the so-called *Monarchomachi*
or " opponents of monarchy " were the Frenchman
Philippe Duplessis-Mornay, and the Scot George
Buchanan. In their works the right of the people to
rebel against their rulers was clearly stated, as was
also the legal obligation of rulers. It was this aspect of
Presbyterianism which led to the opposition of the
English sovereigns to the system. James I summed it
up from the standpoint of the monarch when at the
Hampton Court Conference he said, " You want to
set up a Presbyterian system just as in Scotland.
Now be well assured of this, that such a system has
no more in common with a monarchy than the devil
with God. . . . Every Tom, Dick and Harry would be
free to criticize my policies and short-comings to their
hearts' content."[1]

However, though this may pass as a superficial
judgment it is seen to be far from the truth as soon as
we endeavour to penetrate to the real philosophy
underlying the writings of even the Monarchomachi.
In spite of their readiness for rebellion they still
remained Calvinists, and the conservative element is
never completely overcome. Their republicanism is
not based, for example, on the rights of man as such,
or on the idea of equality. It is thus far removed from
the genuine republicanism which was a later growth.

[1] *v.* M. Piette: *Op. cit.* p. 86.

Nor had these men anything in common with the Levellers. Dryden is wrong when he talks about " their innate antipathy to Kings."[1] The aim always was to establish just such a government as was necessary for the safe-guarding of the Church and promoting the glory of God, as they understood it. Once that is secured then the Calvinists one and all are whole-heartedly on the side of legitimate authority. Nor must it be forgotten that basic in the system was the inequality due to the several divinely or- dained stations or ranks, not to mention the funda- mental difference between the elect and the reprobate. There was in it an aristocratic outlook together with a very firm respect for law and order. So much so, that in spite of all the stimulus it gave to democracy, this conservativism must be regarded rather as the characteristic of the working of the system, taking its history as a whole. However far it has gone in criticizing particular institutions it has always been clear as to the necessity for such institutions, as also it has been equally insistent on the need for the principle of authority in both Church and State. These considerations help us to appreciate the truth of Troeltsch's statement, " All the Calvinistic peoples are characterized by individualism and by democracy, combined with a strong bias towards authority and a sense of the unchangeable nature of law. It is this combination which makes a conservative democracy possible, whereas in Lutheran and Catholic countries, as a matter of course, democracy is forced into an aggressive and revolutionary attitude."[2] Heering, writing of his own country Holland, holds that to-day Neo-Calvinism is socially and politically conservative

[1] *The Hind and the Panther.*   [2] *Op. cit.* p. 619.

having lost its original reforming power.[1] However, it
should be noted in passing that both these writers
agree that Christian socialism sprang up and flourished
just in those sections of the Christian Church which
acknowledged the influence of the Calvinistic tradition.
Thus even amid the conservatism a real concern for
and care of society still remains.

In conclusion we may notice that Calvinism
accepted war as a necessary adjunct to legitimate
authority and even as a means for securing the right
form of government. In spite of the pacifism of
Erasmus, both Luther and Calvin permitted war for
secular purposes of defence provided it is waged with
no confidence in men but with firm trust in God.
The interests of religion, on the contrary, Calvin held
could be promoted only by reliance on God and by
patient endurance and suffering. Later history
showed how utterly impossible it was to make such a
separation between the religious and the secular.
Events seemed to make war necessary and therefore
legitimate, nor was it difficult for Beza to base the
right to make war on the Old Testament Scriptures.

Thus Calvinism as a whole is found on the side of the
authority of the State though reserving a right of
criticism, a conservative force though with many
ideas leading to democracy. It stands for order, but
it would discipline the common man that the order
may be, in part, of his own making, and that at all
times he should feel himself responsible for it. Hence
in the State we have the same principles striving to
work themselves out into permanent arrangements as
were expressed in the theory and life of the Church.
Calvinism is rightly regarded as a specific Church-

[1] G. F. Heering: *The Fall of Christianity*, pp. 101-2.

order moving towards full expression in a Christian civilization. Knox uttered the spirit of the system in his interview with Mary Stuart. " God forbid that I should grasp at the exercise of power or set subjects free to do exactly as they like. My one aim is that Prince and People alike should obey God."[1]

[1] Troeltsch: *Op. cit.* p. 634.

CHAPTER XV

THE REVIVED INTEREST IN CALVINISM

In the course of our survey we have seen that the study of Calvinism brings into focus a number of problems for all of which it offers an attempted solution. In theology such problems as that of the nature of God, His revelation and relationship with men, the place and purpose of the Church and the sacraments: in the ecclesiastical sphere the problem of how to co-ordinate a really strong central authority with the inalienable rights of the people: in sociology the task of fitting the Christian life into the world scheme and regulating all for the glory of God; and in politics the problem of government and the relation of Church and State.

It is seen at a glance that most of these problems are with us to-day, some of them in an acute form. Hence it is not surprising that a growing number of thinkers are turning again to the Reformation period and particularly to Calvinism for help and guidance. Calvin himself is again being read. In Hungary, for example, there has recently appeared a translation of the 1536 edition of the *Institutes*. Also a new French translation has been issued, and the first volume of a German translation. In Holland the Reformed Church has shown fresh activity in issuing handbooks and popular commentaries, with a certain amount of historical work, while scholars in both Germany and France have been turning their attention again to various aspects of the Reformer's work. The interest in Calvin as a man and theologian is evidenced by the

recently published biographies.[1] All this indicates
that Calvinism is by no means a spent force, and
suggests that it has elements of vitality to contribute
to a new era of reconstruction.

In part the revived interest is due to the work of
Karl Barth and the spread of Barthianism throughout the theological world. H. R. Mackintosh speaks
of Barth as " incontestably the greatest figure in
Christian theology that has appeared for decades,"[2]
and it is obviously very significant for the present
influence of Calvinism that Barth and his school find
themselves in agreement with so much of the Reformer's thought. In and through Barth it is found
that many of the fundamental notes of Calvin's
theology are capable of modern statement in such a
way as to win favourable consideration, and the
question inevitably arises whether they are not of
permanent value for Christian thinking.

We are not able here to attempt even a sketch of
Barth's theology, still less an estimate of its value.
But it may be pointed out that in two respects he
shows likeness to Calvin. First in the teaching itself,
the ideas he puts forth and reiterates. And secondly
in his tone and temper. Barth is essentially dogmatic.
He believes in dogma. He puts it forth as dogma.
There is a forthrightness about his assertions with no
apology for his ideas, In this he is, if not actually a
son, at least a kindred spirit of the great Genevan.

And it may well be that the explanation of this
fact is that he, like the Reformer, is elaborating his
position over against the general outlook of his time.

---

[1] *v.* Prof. F. D. Henderson, Article in the *British Weekly*, Sept.
17th, 1936.
[2] *Types of Modern Theology*, p. 263.

Q

Just as Calvin constructed his dogmatic in contra-
distinction to that of the Roman Catholic Church, so
Barth flings out his paradoxes to disturb and shock
the complacency of modern conventional Christianity.
However, as yet, he has not worked out any consistent
dogmatic such as could be compared with that of the
Institutes.

It is, however, a very important point that a
violent reaction from the theology which has gradually developed since the time when Arminianism
triumphed over Calvinism should lead back again in
the direction of the earlier outlook. Not that Arminianism itself is even primarily responsible for the
modern theology which Barth is opposing. But if it
is true that the development which began with
Arminius and which continued throughout the nineteenth century, is now brought to the bar of judgment
and found wanting, then a case is obviously presented
for a new valuation of Calvinism. This seems to be the
effect Barth's work is having. It is bringing some of
Calvin's fundamental ideas again into prominence,
challenging the thought of men with regard to them,
and offering them once more as correctives to the
weakness of the current outlook. It may, of course,
be nothing more than reaction, attractive mainly for
that reason. Whether this is so time alone will show.
But at the moment it is evident that there is here a
power of statement which is capable of striking
into the world of current theological thinking with
disturbing if not quickening power.

We can see the incidence of Barth's challenge as
we mark the features of the theology against
which he revolts. Since Wesley's day there has been a
growing sentimentalism in religion related to the

emphasis on the fatherhood of God and the prominence given to the idea of His love. With this for various reasons has gone the disparagement of dogma in favour of an almost exclusive emphasis on the ethical as against the essentially religious side of Christianity, together with a weakening of the sense of authority, both the authority of God and the authority of dogma. Fitting in with this type of thinking were the social aspirations based on ideas of the rights of man and the equality of all, stimulated by the thin but glowing optimism derived from nineteenth-century idealism, with its strong emphasis on man's moral nature as the mark of his greatness, and the essential rightness of reason and its capacity to serve man adequately in all the emergencies of life. If the outlook is to be summed up in a phrase it is the outlook which makes man the centre of thought rather than God, and which has of necessity unlimited faith in man's ability. This is called humanism, which, it is maintained, has produced an interpretation of Christianity far removed from that of the New Testament.

The main features of this Christian humanism, which if one name above others is to be named can be traced back to the philosophy of Hegel, are the immanence of God even to the loss altogether of the idea of His transcendence; the insistence on the idea that God is discoverable by the processes of human thought, that is, that a way exists from man to God; this leading to the further idea that a careful analysis of religious experience can form an adequate basis of theology.[1] Man is thus in a sense the measure of all things, even of God.

[1] v. E. E. Aubrey: *Present Theological Tendencies*, pp. 61-5.

Against this position the Danish philosopher Kierkegaard revolted and in due time Kierkegaard became the inspiration of Karl Barth.

When it is said that Barth protests against the rock-bottom assumptions of this general attitude it is easy to see the affinity of his mind with that of Calvin. He endeavours to give God again the central and supreme place. He denies that there can be any discovery of God or any knowledge of Him apart from revelation. So he insists that revelation is real and necessary. This revelation is the Word of God and particularly Jesus Christ, but even the Scripture is not revelation until it is made so for each individual by the Holy Spirit. Thus there is an objective authority in the Scriptures though it is not operative till applied by the witness within. Everything connected with salvation is of faith, and faith itself is the gift of God. Barth is as insistent as Calvin on man's total inability. Reason can do nothing for him in this highest realm of the spirit-life. Revelation cannot be tested by it, rather the deliverances of reason itself are tested by the revelation. The God who has spoken, transcendent above all creation and equally above the mind of man, is the one authority, the sole hope of salvation, the Sovereign Lord.

These and other points are elucidated by Barth in such a way that the bare statement of them can be regarded as nothing more than an indication of the general drift of his teaching. It would take many words to do justice to his theology, even if one fully understood it. But his kinship with Calvin is readily discerned. Not of course that he simply revitalizes Calvinism. As far as one can judge the Barthian theology is something different, something new. But

it may be claimed that in a real way the spirit of
Calvinism lives again in it, and is now reappearing
as a quickening force in the thought of men.   It is
easy to see that Calvin's view of the Bible will never
be resuscitated, but it is not certain by any means
that a new conception of biblical authority over the
Christian mind will not emerge, while his doctrine of
the testimony of the Spirit within wins a fresh value as
a starting point for further thinking. Also it is equally
sure that Christian thought will never again put the
Decalogue on a level with the Sermon on the Mount
or use the Old Testament generally in the same naïve
way as the basis of Christian ethics, but on the other
hand Calvin's insistence on the religious as primary is
undoubtedly in the direction of a sound reconstruction.
His idea of authority as an inalienable element of
God's fatherhood, his emphasis on the transcendence
of God, as a corrective to an exaggerated doctrine of
immanence, these are admitted to-day to be valuable
elements.   So too the doctrine of predestination will
hardly be stated again in so rigorous a fashion as by
Calvin, but he would be a bold man who would say
that it is dead and buried. The problem of which it
seeks to be the solution is living wherever God is realized
in His sovereign majesty. Also the disparagement
of reason and the assertion of man's total inability
must, one would think, receive modification, but the
insistence on the fact of divine grace as man's sole
saving power is already winning its way as a corrective
to loose and ineffectual idealism. Deep notes in the
gospel message are being sounded in the Barthian
theology. The fact that these same notes were heard
so clearly in Calvinism reveals the secret of its early
power and of its continuing influence.

It may be noted finally that there are affinities between the spirit and underlying aim of the Barthian theology and the social and political aspirations of the continent of Europe where it was born. There is in it the same pessimism concerning man and society, the same urgent sense of the bankruptcy of human effort, and the same striving after some sure and all-powerful authority. *Tourmenté par un besoin incomparable de certitude* is a phrase applied by Doumergue to Calvin.[1] It would admirably fit both the religious and the political life of to-day. Whether in the immediate future the theological reconstruction which Barth is now offering will meet and come to terms with the political aspirations of the modern world it is impossible to say. But if it should, then we might well see a revived Calvinism forming the theological background of a new constructive era of social and international life.

[1] *Op. cit.* Vol. IV, p. 60.

APPENDIX

ANALYSIS OF THE *INSTITUTES*

A. THE KNOWLEDGE OF GOD AS CREATOR.

   I. From Nature

       (*a*) in creation.

       (*b*) in providence.

              Corruption of reason.

              Necessity of the Scriptures.

              Nature and truth of the Scriptures.

              Their authority.

   II. From the Scriptures

       (*a*) in creation.

              State of man, faculties of the soul, freewill, original righteousness.

       (*b*) in providence.

              General and particular providence.

              The problem of evil.

              The doctrine of God as will.

B. THE KNOWLEDGE OF GOD AS REDEEMER.

           Man's failure. Original sin.

              Corruption of will and intellect.

           Redemption to be sought in Christ.

   I. How Christ is exhibited to us.

       (*a*) in the Old Testament.

              A perfect standard of righteousness in the Law. Exposition of the Decalogue.

       (*b*) in the New Testament.

              Christ as Mediator.

              The two natures in Christ.

              The three offices of the mediator.

              How Christ mediates—the atonement.

II. How Christ is received by us.
> Benefits of Christ made available for us by the Holy Spirit.
>> Faith.
>> Repentance.
>> The life of obedience and self-denial.
>
> Justification by faith.
>> Christian liberty.
>> Prayer. Exposition of Lord's prayer.
>> The eternal election.
>> The last resurrection.

III. How we are retained in the fellowship.
> The nature of the Church.
>> The word.
>> The sacraments.
>> The ministry and government of the Church.
>> Civil government.

INDEX

A

Academy, 143
Adam, 31, 32
America, 158, 163, 164, 172, 175 ff, 226, 234
Anabaptists 70, 115, 130, 151, 205, 225
Andreæ, Valentine, 148
Anhalt-Nassau, 152
Aquinas, 181
Aristotle, 186
Arminianism, 171, 179, 180, 206
Arminius, 96, 153
Arnold, Matthew, 173
Asceticism, 70, 218, 220
Atonement, 55
Augustine, 30, 42, 56, 78, 96, 98, 109, 110
Awakening, the great, 179

B

Baptism, 101, 112 ff.
  Infant, 115 ff.
Baptists, 171
Barth, Karl, 241 ff.
Baxter, 170, 225, 228
Belief, 65
Belloc, Hilaire, 223
Bernard, St., 78
Beza, 150, 236
Bible, 181 ff., 195, 197
  Genevan, 166
Bohemia, 152, 159
Bossuet, 134
Brandenburg, 152
Bremen, 152
Bucer, Martin, 166
Buchanan, George, 236
Bullinger, 150
Bunyan, 77, 174, 205

C

Calling, 211, 221
  effectual, 94
Camillus, 41
Capitalism, 222 ff.
Carolina, 180
Carrickfergus, 165
Cartwright, Thomas, 167
Castellion, 205
Catechism, 142
  for children, 151, 152, 162
  Heidelberg, 153
  Larger and Shorter, 168, 180
Ceremonies, 68
Charity, 83, 106
Charles I, 186
Church, 99 ff.
  of England, 166, 167, 171
  government of, 130 ff.
  invisible, 100
  Reformed Dutch, 181
  Reformed, of U.S.A., 181
  Roman Catholic, 30, 62, 70, 76, 81, 129, 138, 185, 227
  and State, 141 ff.
  unity of, 103, 131
  visible, 101, 102
Chrysostom, 144
Commandments, 48
Communion of saints, 101, 104
Confessio Gallica, 157, 159
Confession
  Belgic, 153, 154
  Heidelberg, 151
  Scotch, 161
  Second Helvetic, 151
  Waldensian, 159
  Westminster, 161, 168, 180, 201
  Zurich, 151
  of sins, 71, 111
Congregation, Lords of, 160

249